The Tenth Muse:

How Maria Antonia Advanced the Pastoral Opera

April Lynn James

The Tenth Muse: How Maria Antonia Advanced the Pastoral Opera

For more information, email aprilplusmadison@gmail.com.

ISBN: 979-8-89109-006-4 - paperback
ISBN: 979-8-89109-007-1 - ebook
ISBN: 979-8-89109-193-1 - hardcover

FIND YOUR VOICE!

Do you have a dream that you're longing to bring to fruition, but something keeps stopping you? Are you living your life with intention and purpose? Do you long to be seen and heard?

Download my complimentary e-book, *Finding Your Voice: 5 Keys to Unlock Your Natural Self-Esteem* and discover five practices that you can implement TODAY to start manifesting the life you are meant to live. Just one click for five tips!

Go to https://tinyurl.com/2p8ez3fa and get your five keys today!

You can also get a copy by visiting:

www.aprilplusmadison.com

Contents

Acknowledgements

To all those acknowledged at the front of my dissertation, those thanks still apply. For this book, I would additionally like to thank the following institutions and individuals without whom this work would have remained just another unpublished dissertation:

Karin Graf, Heidrun Lange, and Barbara Andersson of the Staatliche Kunstsammlungen Dresden for their help in obtaining permission to publish the photo of the portrait of Maria Antonia of Bavaria.

Dr. Steve Turley, through whom I found out about Chandler Bolt and Self-Publishing School.

All the coaches, staff, and Mastermind Community of SPS, and to my editor, Sandra Wissinger.

I also want to thank my family and friends—those who are still among us in the physical as well as those who have shuffled off this mortal coil—for their continued love and encouragement.

Thank you, BG.

And lastly, but certainly not leastly, thanks be to God.

Letter to the Reader

Nearly two decades ago, my elevator pitch sounded something like this: "Hi, I'm Dr. April Lynn James and I'm the founder of the Maria Antonia Project, an opera company dedicated to bringing operas composed by women out of the archives and onto the stage." This statement would inevitably be met with the question: "Were there any operas composed by women?" This book is one of the answers to this question.

When I set out to research women composers, I had no idea that I would wind up writing the first comprehensive English-language biography of Maria Antonia Walpurgis Symphorosa (1724-1780), Electress of Saxony, a multitalented noblewoman who lived in the German states of the Holy Roman Empire in the mid-18th century during a period of constantly shifting political alliances, but I am glad I did. Studying Her Highness helped me to not only improve my understanding of 18th-century music and history, but it also helped me to better understand myself.

A native New Yorker, I had spent my undergraduate years at Queens College of the City University of New York, a public college.

Dissuaded from majoring in music by parents who did not consider a music degree to be "practical," I earned a BA in communications and an MA in media studies, then worked diligently but unhappily in publishing and television for two years. I consulted many career guides, and my heart, during that time. When I was laid off the day before Thanksgiving 1992, I decided to return to Queens College to study my first love, music. By this time, I had become fascinated by 18th-century music, and along the way, I also became interested in researching female composers due to the distinct lack of works by women in the music history textbooks, concerts, and culture of the time. This was the early 1990s, where people knew about Hildegard von Bingen (12th century) and Clara Schumann (19th century)—that was about it. I found it hard to believe that no woman had created or published music during the intervening centuries, so I started investigating. Since I'm a singer, a soprano, I decided to focus on vocal music and opera, with the hope that, through specializing in this repertory, I could forge a career in a very competitive field.

I wanted to go directly into a PhD program, but it turned out that I had not taken enough music courses as an undergraduate. In order to pursue a PhD in Music, I would need to earn a second BA in the subject. So, that's what I did, defying parental pressure. Once I started getting straight As as well as scholarships and fellowships, they came around. Then I got into Harvard, and that really sealed the deal.

But studying at the Big H was not at all like studying at QC. At this old private university, status games were *de rigueur*. As an adult student, I had been on a first-name basis with my professors at QC, but at Harvard, a first-year graduate student was at the bottom of the pecking order. We would not be allowed to address our professors by their first names until after we passed our general exams in our third year. The whole process of graduate school was unnecessarily competitive and stressful, and not just for me. During our orientation week, Residential Advisors and other staff spoke about the suicide rate and the services that were in place to help prevent such things.

Still, I persevered. I like to think that Maria Antonia chose me to write this dissertation on her because the process happened quite organically. I took a class called Manuscript Sources at Harvard. The professor—Christoph Wolff, who would later become my dissertation advisor—had pulled various scores from the library shelves for the class and laid them on a table. As I looked at them, one caught my eye because it was by a woman. It turned out to be the second and third acts from Maria Antonia's opera, *Il trionfo della fedeltà*. I asked him, "Is anyone working on her?" He said, "No," to which my immediate response was, "I am now."

Thus began a wonderful journey through time and culture that broadened my horizons and called upon many of my favorite skills. It gave me a chance to use the French I'd learned as a child and in high school, the German I had begun studying in college, and the Italian I'd begun studying as part of my second BA. These were the three languages that I would need in order to do my research: the language of 18th-century court society was French, the language of opera and much of Maria Antonia's poetry was Italian, and the research language of musicology was German.

My doctoral years also set the stage for my current work: helping people recover their joy and sense of purpose so that they can live healthier and happier lives. During my second year of grad school, I developed a repetitive strain injury in my right arm from sitting in the library working on my computer all the time. Due to stress, I gained weight, going up one whole dress size, and was terribly unhappy. I realized that I needed to get out of the music department, away from my computer, and, above all, away from the stressful, hypercompetitive environment.

I got moving. I took modern dance on Radcliffe's campus and baroque dance at the Longy School of Music, the conservatory just down the street from Harvard. I took mime classes with an independent teacher from Bulgaria. I got back into juggling—a skill I had learned to stave off boredom during my TV days—and joined the Harvard Juggling Club, even though graduate students were not allowed to be official members of an undergraduate club. I continued singing and taking voice lessons, though stress made singing freely nearly impossible. I got back into yoga and took up Alexander Technique and Feldenkrais to better understand my body. Basically, I did anything and everything I could to get myself out of a negative environment and to cultivate positive relationships with people outside of school, with creatives rather than intellectuals.

It paid off. I returned to my normal dress size and the tendinitis went away. Thus, the seeds of my PLAY Elements were sown.

"What are the PLAY Elements?" you might ask. Why, they are the distillation of everything I have learned about what it takes to navigate the twists and turns of life with one's sense of humor and health intact (with a good deal of *Alice in Wonderland*-inspired whimsy thrown in for good measure). P stands for Positivi-Tea & Perseverance—using positive affirmations to help heal mind and body; L is for Love and Laugh—focusing on what you love and enjoying the process; A is for Awe & Authentici-Tea—getting in touch with feelings of wonder by getting out into nature and uncovering one's authentic desires by connecting to divine guidance using astrology; Y is for staying Young-at-Heart through Youth-Enhancing Movement, maintaining the flexibili-Tea of our analog bodies in a digital environment.

I kept PLAY-ing during my fourth year of grad school when I happily embarked upon a research year in Dresden, Germany.

Even though I spent most of my time in the Sächsisches Landes-und Universitätsbibliothek or Hauptstaatsarchiv, I made time to continue studying mime at Mimenstudio Dresden. I continued private voice study, and I took time to travel around Europe, for research and for pleasure. Because my baroque dance studies had improved my understanding of 18th-century culture in a way that simple book learning never could, I strove to see and hear Dresden, Munich, Padua, Prague, and other locations the way Maria Antonia might have. After returning to the US, I spent two years writing the present work and then became the first graduate student to perform as part of a Music Department dissertation presentation. I got my degree in June 2002 and remained in Cambridge for another year, working part time at Harvard's Loeb Music Library.

I was in the right place at the right time. They had just inherited a collection of opera scores, and a significant portion of these works were by women. I was asked to curate an exhibit using these resources, and thus *In Her Own Hand: Operas Composed by Women 1625-1913* was born. It was the first exhibit in an American library on this topic and remained on display for well over a year. Maria Antonia was one of the eighteen composers featured.

I had combined that job with part-time work as a juggler in a touring educational show, but after a year, I was burnt out. Combining two part-time jobs into one was not my idea of a satisfying postdoc life. I returned to NYC, bringing my research with me, and founded the Maria Antonia Project.

I spent the better part of a decade recovering from my graduate school experience. I have come to refer to this time as my Decade of Awfulness because, while life may have unfolded the way it was supposed to, it definitely did not unfold according to my plans. I struggled to get the company off the ground in New York's hypercompetitive environment while attending to my increasingly health-challenged mother. Although my brother's return to the family abode in 2012 was problematic, it gave me the impetus I needed to escape from an intractable situation, put the Maria Antonia Project on hiatus, and move to Philadelphia in 2013, where my research on women composers eventually found a more receptive audience at the University of Pennsylvania. *In Her Own Hand* lives on as a LibGuide accessible through the Penn Libraries website, partly fulfilling a wish I had had since the exhibit's creation.

So, after all that, why publish this book now? In part, it is because my research on Maria Antonia is still a solid contribution to the fields of music history, women's history, German cultural studies, opera, and arts and literature, even though it was completed twenty years ago. Publishing it now gives me a chance to correct a few points I had made back in 2002 in light of my improved understanding of operatic performance. I have been further encouraged by the responses to my research of female artists and entrepreneurs I work with who have a genuine hunger for the knowledge contained within these pages. I also want to give hope and inspiration to the alt-academic community, those of us with doctorates seeking to forge satisfying careers and lives outside the academy. Furthermore, making my book available in e-book and print-on-demand form serves my desire to get my research out of the ivory tower.

What you will find here:

- *Chapter 1: Court as Theater and Theater at Court* is a summary of the research that had been conducted on Maria Antonia up through 2002, and an outline of the theoretical background of my book.
- *Chapter 2: The Princess' Musical Influences* is a look at what Maria Antonia's music catalogs can tell us about her musical education.
- *Chapter 3: Maria Antonia's Artistry Gains Recognition* is a biography of the first thirty years of Maria Antonia's life and

contextualizes her music and poetry as part of a court society that valued Italian culture over earlier French models.

- *Chapter 4: The Music and Poetry of Maria Antonia's Youth* examines some of Her Highness' earliest poetry: six arias and cantatas texts that were set to music by Johann Adolf Hasse and Giovanni Ristori. These sources are analyzed for the first time, allowing us to gain a more complete understanding of Maria Antonia's style and compositional choices.

- *Chapter 5: Opera Seria, Intermezzo, or Pastoral?* looks at Maria Antonia's literary influences and gives the reader a glimpse into the early 18th-century music-theatrical landscape.

- *Chapter 6: Her First Opera: Il trionfo della fedeltà* is an in-depth examination of this work, again using sources hitherto unexamined. I argue, in opposition to previous researchers, that the work is solely that of Maria Antonia. I look at how she inserts herself into the genre of the pastoral opera (with its shepherds and shepherdesses) by playing a heroine who is active. She is not in need of rescue but rather, through mercy, compassion, and steadfastness, rescues the hero.

- *Chapter 7: Her Highness' Voice* answers the question, "What did Maria Antonia sound like?" and looks at what happened to her first opera when it reached Vienna.

- *Chapter 8: The Princess and the Enlightenment* examines Maria Antonia in the public sphere by drawing upon primary sources such as letters to furnish an understanding of why and how a woman of her station would publish her works. It also examines the connections between Her Highness and Enlightenment writer Luise Gottsched.

- *Chapter 9: The Seven Years' War and Beyond* fleshes out the biography of Maria Antonia's last twenty-four years.

I conclude the book with three appendices: the first one is a listing of all illustrations that have been provided in the book; the second one is a comprehensive listing of both Maria Antonia's works and primary sources relating to her; the third one is a listing of composers whose works were a treasured part of Maria Antonia's library. Again, most of these sources had been unexamined by previous researchers. Additionally, English-language descriptions of the majority had been unavailable to scholars.

May you enjoy getting to know Her Highness, her music, and her world as much as I have.

Introduction

My study of Maria Antonia Walpurgis Symphorosa (1724-1780), Princess of Bavaria and later Electress of Saxony, is the story of the trials and tribulations of a highly talented woman who lived during a period of constantly shifting political alliances that characterized life in the German states of the Holy Roman Empire in the mid-18th century. This period is also known to history as the Enlightenment. It was a time which questioned the rights and roles of hereditary rulers and the relation of women and men to the cosmos, society, and one another. It was also a time of nascent nationalism. The effect of these crosscurrents on the arts, and on their representative and patron, Maria Antonia, cannot be underestimated.

An understanding of her life and works requires a knowledge of and contributes to several fields beyond music history: German history, the history of the Enlightenment, and literary history. Let me describe the contributions to each of these in turn.

Most German histories of Germany have been written from a Prussian point of view. This is due, in part, to the bias of 19th-century historians toward the German state of their birth. Though claiming objectivity, the historians of the 19th century generally have a very real Prussian bias, and the nationalism of the time tended to subsume all the achievements of the different states into that of a single, unified Germany, a nation which, it must be remembered, did not come into being until 1871.

The push toward unity was led by Prussia in a continuation of policies set in motion by Frederick II in the 18th century, and the "Prussianization" of German history could be said to have started with Frederick's wars against Saxony and Austria.[1] These general histories emphasize war and large, life-changing political events. They are often devoid of considerations of cultural life, and rarely include women as anything but minor figures.[2]

Historians of the Enlightenment have tended to dismiss the early and middle 18th century to focus on the later 18th and early 19th centuries, for which historical records are more complete.[3] The period from 1700 through 1763 is a time of economic and political upheaval. Let us remember that it is only a century following the devastation of the Thirty Years' War (1618-1648). For a cultural historian, it is still a time when gaping holes exist.

A century was not enough to repair all the disruptions by the time renewed wars broke out in the 1740s. Many cultural institutions were in the process of being rebuilt or were just being created. Still,

---

1 In German history texts, these are referred to as the Silesian Wars, which include the Seven Years' War. For a summary of German historical literature, see Gagliardo, *Germany under the Old Regime 1600-1790,* and regarding the changes in the Holy Roman Empire, see also his *Reich Nation*

2 Gagliardo, to his credit, does devote three chapters to various cultural developments in the German states. See G*ermany under the Old Regime.*

3 For more on this, see Umbach, *Federalism and Enlightenment in Germany, 1740-1806,* and Gagliardo, *Old Regime.*

histories of the Enlightenment tend to focus on the literary and scientific achievements of men, and most of these histories deal in great detail with English or French cultural models. The little that has been done on German sources focuses on figures such as Goethe or Kant. Only now, with the dissolution of the Soviet Union and freer access to archival materials, have researchers begun to look into Saxony and its contributions to the artistic and scientific achievements of the age.

Music history as it has been taught too often focuses on names and events, and its creation of a past that in linear fashion leads from the Dorian scale to minimalism is seen increasingly as antiquated.[4] Standard histories of music are based on a 19th-century view of creativity, which tends to restrict this activity to certain gifted individuals. It is a view which privileged the professional composer and musician over the amateur, and which tended to set the composer above the culture in which s/he lived. It is also a view of history that privileged the accomplishments of men (in the "public" sphere) over those of women (in the "private" sphere). This distinction between public and private spheres could not and has not put women's accomplishments on an equal footing with men's.[5]

Starting in the 1970s, spurred by civil rights and feminist movements, scholars began to re-examine the conventional historical methodology. Women's studies began to come into its own as a discipline, and many scholars began the long overdue work of locating female predecessors. This had a revolutionary effect on literary studies, and these successes affected music historians. The 1980s saw a steady growth in research and writing about female composers. The groundbreaking work by the contributors to *Women Making Music* paved the

---

4 See such works as Grout and Palisca's *A History of Western Music* for the linear style of music history research.

5 See Citron, *Gender and the Musical Canon* chapters 3 and 4 for a discussion of how the concepts of creativity and of professionalism have been used to dismiss women's accomplishments.

way for a wholesale revamping of the Western art music tradition. At last, scholars were starting to look at the traditional bastions of power and tradition—church and court—to see what their women were doing.

The many studies that have followed in recent years are a wonderful treasure trove of information. They do, however, have their limitations as far as the present study is concerned. Work on women in German-speaking lands is largely missing. This is as true in enlightenment histories as it is in music histories.[6] Literary histories are generally biased toward English and French resources; music histories have focused on Italy. The very titles of these works show that the authors would like to generalize about women's aesthetics or perspectives throughout history; however, this is not possible when large sections of the historical puzzle are still missing.

New work by several Germanists is beginning to plug these holes in our cultural landscape. There have been works such as *Deutsche Literatur von Frauen* which have begun to restore work by German women from the Middle Ages to the 20th century to the cultural landscape. There are also a growing number of German American literary historians who have begun offering works by German women in translation. *Bitter Healing*, an anthology of writings by German women from 1700-1830, is one example.

As the authors point out, in the field of German literature, women authors have been more consistently excluded from the canon than their sisters in England.[7] In music history, most female composers from all countries are still excluded from the canon, although a few

---

6 See, for example, *Women's Poetry in the Enlightenment*, which deals exclusively and un-apologetically with British writers. In *Women Making Music* and *Women in Music*, it is either in the Middle Ages that German women are discussed (Hildegard von Bingen) or in the Classical and Romantic periods (Luise Reichardt, Clara Schumann, Fanny Hensel).
7 Blackwell and Zantop, *Bitter Healing*, p. 1.

are increasingly included in the textbooks and in concert programs.[8] Many women composed for their religious institutions (Hildegard von Bingen, Isabella Leonarda), or for secular academies and salons (Barbara Strozzi, Fanny Mendelssohn). There are practically no female composers of opera mentioned in the standard texts.[9] This is where my study of Maria Antonia can be particularly valuable. It restores to us a voice long silent.

My research has focused on the resources of two Dresden archives: the Hauptstaatsarchiv (HStA) and the Sächsische Landes- und Universitätsbibliothek (SLUB). I also conducted some research in Berlin and Munich, Germany, in Vienna, Austria, and in Padova, Italy. Major losses were sustained by the German libraries during World War II, making the verification of certain details from previous biographies difficult, and in many cases, impossible. However, there is still much to be found. An overview is necessary because of the complexity of the task.

The earliest biographical sources on Maria Antonia are articles in two 18th-century lexica: Peter Paul Finauer's *Allgemeines Historisches Verzeichniss gelehrter Frauenzimmer* Bd. I (1761) and Ernst Ludwig Gerber's *Historisch-Biographisches Lexicon der Tonkünstler* (1790). Finauer was the author of several books and lexica, all dealing with some aspect of Bavarian history. It is therefore not surprising that

---

8 Hildegard von Bingen (1098-1179), Barbara Strozzi (1619-1664), Elisabeth Claude Jacquet de la Guerre (1665-1729), Fanny Mendelssohn (1805-1847) and Clara Schumann (1819-1896) are the female pre-20th-century composers that are to be seen regularly in textbooks. See chapter 1 of Citron, *Gender and the Musical Canon* for a discussion of the issues surrounding the canonization of music.

9 Elisabeth-Claude Jacquet de la Guerre is known to have written one opera, *Cephale et Procris*. Before her, Francesca Caccini (1587-after 1644) wrote *La liberazione di Ruggiero dall'isola d'Alcina* (1625) for the Medici court in Florence. Contemporary with Maria Antonia was Maria Teresa Agnesi of Milan who achieved some public and professional success with her productions of *Il re pastore* and other works. For the standard historicization of music, see Donald J. Grout and Claude V. Palisca's A *History of Western Music*. For more on women as composers of opera, see *Women Composers Through the Ages* and articles on the above-mentioned composers in the *New Grove Dictionary of Women Composers*.

Maria Antonia should have a prominent place in his general history of learned women. Gerber's article is short, with mention of the operas, Maria Antonia's skill as a singer and keyboardist (apparently drawn from Burney), and her Arcadian Academy connection. It adds no new information to what can be found in Finauer, and it erroneously states the year of her death as 1782.

The mid-19th century saw a revival of interest in Maria Antonia, due mainly to the interest of the Bavarian state government, which is to say, the Bavarian royal family. In 1854, it expressed to the Saxon government the wish to make public historical materials dealing with the life history of Maria Antonia. This was at the behest of King Max II. Joseph, who came into power in 1848 with the desire, inherited from his father, to make the artistic and scientific achievements of Bavaria and of Germany, from every epoch, known throughout the world.[10]

Consequently, in that same year, an article appeared on Maria Antonia in *Geschichte der deutschen Höfe des Hauses Sachsen* by E. Vehse. This was followed by an article by Eduard Bernsdorf in his 1857 *Universal-Lexikon der Tonkunst*. Bernsdorf's short entry appears to be based upon the Gerber lexicon. The wish of the Bavarian government bore substantial fruit, however, in the first book-length biography on Maria Antonia by Carl von Weber, Director of the Hauptstaatsarchiv Dresden in 1857. Entitled *Maria Antonia Walpurgis, Churfürstin zu Sachsen, geb. Kaiserliche Prinzessin in Bayern,* Weber's tome published hithertofore unknown documents, mostly letters, for the first time. It seems to be a fairly trustworthy and unbiased account of her life, even considering that Weber was, to a greater or lesser extent, working for King Johann of Saxony.

A similarly titled bibliography of works by and associated with Maria Antonia by Julius Petzholdt, Director of the Royal Library,

---

10 See Lippert, *Kaiserin Maria Theresia und Kurfürstin Maria Antonia von Sachsen: Brief-wechsel 1747-1772,* p. XI.

also appeared in 1857. It is subtitled *Ein Beitrag zu einer Deutschen Nationalliteratur.* The titles of these volumes show an awareness of the need to create a unified German nation and history, a need whose seeds had been sown a century earlier.

These sources do not, however, deal adequately with the musical and literary materials they mention, since they are intended to be more general histories of their subject.

Another 19th-century source is an article in the *Wissenschaftliche Beilage der Leipziger Zeitung,* which is a summary, clarification, and review of Weber's book. Fürstenau published his own history of music at the Dresden court, *Zur Geschichte der Musik und des Theaters am Hofe zu Dresden,* in 1862. It is a comprehensive survey of music at the court of Saxony from the Renaissance through Baroque periods, but unfortunately, over a century later, Fürstenau's book is still the only exhaustive study of this subject. It is also incomplete, as he died before writing a second volume, which would have covered music from the Baroque period into the 19th century. Furthermore, although he was a musician at court, and thus had access to the materials of the royal library, in my opinion and that of other researchers, Fürstenau was not always the most able interpreter of the information available.

Heinz Drewes' 1934 dissertation, *Maria Antonia Walpurgis als Komponistin* seeks to prove the authorship of Maria Antonia's operas—a question left open by Weber. It does so by comparing the instrumentation, the thematic and harmonic structure of her arias to those of Johann Adolf Hasse, who is thought to have been Maria Antonia's composition teacher in Dresden. His study is flawed by a reliance on Weber and Fürstenau when it comes to verifying or disputing the composition of music by the Electress. Moreover, in dealing only with the operas, he fails to create a complete understanding of the development of her style. Drewes' study is also marred by a view of amateur music production which is condescending at best, and not atypical of the Nazi era in its dismissal of women as composers.

On the heels of the Second World War, there appears a study of Maria Antonia by Alan Yorke-Long in his book, *Music at Court: Four Eighteenth Century Studies.* In four articles of roughly equal length, it examines the musical life of Frederick II, King of Prussia, Maria Antonia, the rulers of the Duchy of Parma, and Charles Eugene, Duke of Württemberg. This has remained, until now, the only in-depth examination of Maria Antonia available in English. The book was compiled from fragments after Yorke-Long's untimely death in 1952.

From its introduction, written by Edward Dent, it is marred by assumptions typical of musicological research in the 1950s and of British musicological research in general.[11] It is anti-Italian opera (Dent calls the productions for the Hapsburgs in Vienna "operatic monstrosities"); it sees the interests of the nobility in creative endeavors as "frivolous;" it disdains the vital contributions of singers to the opera of the period, claiming they had too much influence in the creation of the operas in which they performed; and it does not take the creativity of women seriously. Instead of attempting to meet 18th-century culture on its own terms, Yorke-Long looks down his nose at absolutist European society as a whole.

From start to finish, the article on Maria Antonia is contemptuous in tone. It seems unlikely that Yorke-Long conducted any independent archival research, given the state of the German libraries in the early postwar period. His study relies too heavily upon Weber and Fürstenau for its facts and assumptions, contributing little in the way of original research. Moreover, there is no bibliography, and factual errors are plentiful.

---

11   Even 19th-century works such as those by Vernon Lee have this dismissive attitude towards music emanating from continental Europe.

As for the later 20th century, occasional mention of Maria Antonia has been made in articles on women composers and in books on the Saxon royal family. There is even an entry on Maria Antonia in the *New Grove*. All seem to rely upon the previously mentioned sources.

In the Sächsische Landesbibliothek and in the Hauptstaatsarchiv, there exist approximately 35 poems dedicated to Maria Antonia dated 1747 and 1780.[12] From these, one can chart her life from her arrival in Dresden and marriage into the Saxon royal family, through visits to castles throughout Saxony, to congratulations on births, to wishes of good health for her name and birthdays (June 13 and July 18 respectively), to celebration of her musical and poetic talents, and, finally, to the mourning of her death. These prints are from a variety of authors, and all but one are from men. These men are professors and students at the universities of Leipzig and Wittenberg (the main academies in Saxony), priests, fellow members of the Arcadian Academy, members of the Accademici Filarmonici of Verona, and ordinary citizens. Many are in Latin (such as *Concordia Pax et Amor*), some are in Italian, but most are in German.

Journal articles from the 18th century on Maria Antonia's creative endeavors are relatively rare. Two articles in *Journal Étranger* from May 1755 and January 1756 discuss her first opera, *Il trionfo della fedeltà*, and compare her poetry favorably to that of Metastasio. The 1756 *Journal* Étranger, in addition, published an aria from *Trionfo*. Mention is made in 1763 in the *Dresdner Merkwürdigkeiten* and the *Sächsisches Curiositäten-Cabinet* of performances of her second opera, *Talestri*. All of these were monthly publications, available for purchase by anyone, which reported on the comings and goings of the nobility and members of court.

---

12 See listing in Appendix 1.

There are also numerous musical works dedicated to the Princess. Most of them come from musicians in her circle: Giovanni Ferrandini, Nicola Porpora, Giovanni Alberto Ristori, Johann Adolf Hasse, and Padre Martini. Other dedicators include Wilhelm Friedemann Bach, the opera composer Maria Teresa Agnesi, and the Saxon Princes and Princesses. One very interesting work is *Detail d'un divertissement, donné le dernier jour de carnaval 1763. à S.A.R. Madame la princesse electorale de sax*e, by Count de Marainville, brigadier and envoy to the imperial army stationed in Saxony. This print is a summary of the stage action and a complete copy of the text and music for a 1763 performance in Maria Antonia's honor, at which she was installed as the Tenth Muse. It is a fascinating glimpse into the performance traditions at court.

Also an interesting musical source are the six masses by Johann Schürer, court composer, for Saint Anthony of Padua. Saint Anthony was Maria Antonia's (and her mother's) patron saint. There is one mass for each year from 1758-64, with the exception of 1759 (the year that the royal family fled for safety to Munich). These Catholic masses open a window into the performance practices of the royal church.

Dedications of music to Maria Antonia from her own children offer insights into their education. Friedrich August, her firstborn, was known as a keyboardist; her fourth son Anton was a composer; and Maximilian, her fifth son, inherited his mother's poetic talents. Anton's musical works fill fifty volumes in the Landesbibliothek. He wrote versions of arias from his mother's two operas and dedicated an intermezzo to her. Often Anton and Maximilian worked together on such musical works.[13]

A non-musical work dedicated to the Electress is the collection of letters to and from the playwright and translator Luise Gottsched.

---

13 See Landmann, "Gli amanti folletti- ein Dresdener Mozart-Pasticcio."

The editor, Dorothee Henriette v. Runckel specifically mentions Maria Antonia in the dedication to *Briefe der Frau Luise Adelgunde Victorie Gottsched geborne Kalmus*. Maria Antonia's name also appears at the top of the list of subscribers for the third volume of these letters. Her son, Friederich August, Elector of Saxony, is listed second.

Previously unexamined sources are catalogs of the libraries belonging to Maria Antonia and other members of the court. This includes the *Catalogo de[i] Libri Numerati Musicali d[e] S[on] A[ltesse] R[oyale] M[aria] A[ntonia] D[ux] de B[avarie]*. (after 1746), and the *Catalogus, von Ihro Königliche Hoheit der weÿland Durchlauchtigsten, Fürstin und Frau Frau Maria Antonia, verwittibten Chufürstin zu Sachsen, gebohrnen Römisch Kaÿserlichen Prinzessin und Herzogin in Ober und Nieder-Bayern, Bibliotheck nebst denen Preissen, zum XXIsten Capitel des Haupt-Inventarii gehörig*. (c. 1780). The first of these is a seemingly thorough list of all the scores that Maria Antonia brought with her from Munich, many of which are still extant. The second catalog consists of Maria Antonia's non-musical library, which contained over 3,000 books at the time of her death. In it are books in several European languages and Latin, and on topics from literature to theology. Although it is probable that some portion of this library consists of books that she inherited from her spouse, the glimpse it gives into her educational background is invaluable.

Visual sources offer a glimpse into Maria Antonia's life that is often missing from written sources. Several portraits of her and of members of her family are extant. The best-known official ones are the formal court portrait by the court painter Anton Raphael Mengs (1751) and the less formal portrait painted by the principal court painter, Pietro Graf Rotari, in 1755. Both are still on view in the Gemäldegalerie Alte Meister in Dresden. There exist, in addition, self-portraits by Maria Antonia, and engravings of her as frontispieces to prints of her operas. Copies of her portraits were sent to different courts—to family members and to political allies—as gifts, which has led to their dispersal throughout Germany and Europe.

Perhaps the richest source of information on Maria Antonia and other members of the royal family is their correspondence. The Hauptstaatsarchiv contains thousands of letters to and from Maria Antonia, her spouse, her mother-in-law and her father-in-law (the King and Queen), et al. Some of these were excerpted in 1908 by Woldemar Lippert in *Kaiserin Maria Theresia und Kurfürstin Maria Antonia von Sachsen Briefwechsel 1747-1772*. The relationship between the Empress and her cousin makes for interesting reading, and for wonderful insights into both women's characters. It also contradicts the view put forth in *New Grove* that Maria Antonia experienced increasing "personal and artistic isolation" after becoming the Electress Dowager.

Also in HStA is a document that, until recently, was in France. *Das geheime politische Tagebuch des Kurprinzen Friedrich Christian 1751-1757* (finally published in 1992) provides information not available to previous biographers. In addition to descriptions of political goings-on, the Prince mentions details of family life. That the love and respect Maria Antonia had for him was returned wholeheartedly can be surmised by the frequent references to her as a "zweite ich" and other such statements. In fact, this document shows more clearly than any other that Friedrich Christian viewed Maria Antonia very much as an equal political partner. My study looks at how the tensions between Maria Antonia's public and private roles affected her creative journey.

The musical and poetic works from Maria Antonia include her operas *Il trionfo della fedeltà* and *Talestri, regina delle amazzoni*, as well as a set of arias and several cantata texts based on pastoral themes, books of poetry, books on religious subjects, an oratorio text *La conversione di Sant'Agostino*, and two works of fiction. Maria Antonia was considered a remarkable talent in her own time for being equally adept at the composition of music and poetry. Conventional music history teaches that it was only in the 19th century, in the person of Richard Wagner, that the ideal of a composer/producer/librettist in one person was reached. Clearly this teaching will need to be revised as it was in the 18th century through women such as Maria Antonia that this ideal was first reached.[14]

The standard musical and literary histories have too often ghettoized women's accomplishments[15] and have created a sort of canon mirroring men's work. This book shows how Maria Antonia's contributions to culture were part of a larger cultural discourse. Women and men traded ideas and learned from one another, and it is only the writers of history (largely men) who have done history a great disservice by seeing women's work as unimportant or inferior. To paraphrase Blackwell and Zantop, although music historians have often assumed that women "inspired" male composers and then "copied" or "trivialized" men's lofty innovations, a look at the music and poetry associated with Maria Antonia suggests the reverse: she created new themes or revised the conception of old ones, which were then adopted by men or claimed as their own.[16]

What mars 19th- and 20th-century biographies on 18th-century Europe in general is a refusal to try to understand the culture of the Baroque period on its own terms. As a performer of early music—as a singer, dancer, and theater artist—and as one who has studied the dances, the operas, and the etiquette of the period, I hope to be able to come closer to giving an accurate picture of the world surrounding Maria Antonia than her previous biographers have done.

---

14 Wilhelmina von Bayreuth, sister of Frederick II, composed the text and music for at least one opera performed at her court in 1740.

15 An example being the *New Grove Dictionary of Women Composers*.

16 *Bitter Healing*, p. 2.

By looking at the artifacts from this past culture, I hope to provide a perspective that will broaden the research of this period and move the teaching of music history away from a focus on "Great Composers." To look at composers as somehow above the circumstances of their period, and to characterize music as progressing in a linear fashion towards some goal intuited only by the "greats" is to divorce the music and composers from their own place and time.

Although one cannot literally visit the past, I have sought, through its artifacts—scores, books, libretti, letters, dedications, paintings, and diaries—and through visits to sites important to my study—Dresden, Leipzig, Meissen, Munich, Vienna, Prague, Berlin, and points around and in between—to envision Maria Antonia's world.[17] Though much changed by the ravages of time and warfare, these sites still yielded a wealth of information.

A word on naming: women's history scholars have rightly regarded the names women bear as a subject for study.[18] I have chosen to refer to my subject throughout the book as "Maria Antonia" and not, as the *New Grove* might put it, "Maria Antonia Walpurgis" or as simply "Walpurgis." My reasoning is simple: this is how my subject referred to herself. It was followed by whatever title she had at the time from "Dux (de) Bavariae" to "Princesse Royal" to "Kurfürstin Witwe," but "Maria Antonia" is the only title she had that stayed consistent from the beginning to the end of her life. That she recognized this can be seen in those books in Dresden which still bear her monogram. It reads "MA" and is surmounted by a crown.

---

17 Even porcelain turns out to be of use in understanding the loves of this culture. More than just pretty dishes, porcelain is a window into the cultural history that is too easily overlooked. The importance of commedia dell'arte, the honoring of important people (i.e., the nobility), the portrayal of women and men's roles, the portrayal of racial and ethnic minorities—each of these are fascinating chapters of history that can be told through looking at this one artifact.

18 See Citron, *Gender*, pp. 97-100. Also Kord, *Little Detours*, pp. 132-138.

Furthermore, when dealing with research on a member of the nobility, it is important to remember the ways in which they distinguished themselves from the rest of society. One of these ways was in their lack of what we call last names. Nobles had their family names of course: Maria Antonia was a Wittelsbach and married into the Wettin family. However, in normal usage, these names were not equivalent to "Smith" or "Jones," and were not used in that way. Royalty were referred to by their dynastic connections, and these connections were more visible in their given names and in their titles.

Therefore, throughout my study, I will refer to my subject as she referred to herself, by her given name and by her titles. Variously, she is Maria Antonia, or the Princess, or the Princess Royal, or the Electress, or the Electress Dowager. This gives her an equality of status with the others of her class: her spouse Friedrich Christian, her mother Maria Amalia, her father Karl Albrecht, her mother-in-law (and aunt) Maria Josepha, her father-in-law Friedrich August II and so on. This is not to create confusion, but to help one see the stages of her life and her changing relationship to herself and others.

My study shows that the life of any creative person, as in that of Maria Antonia, cannot be understood in isolation from the lives of those around them. Maria Antonia's story also illustrates the complex negotiations women have historically had to make in order to have their voices heard.[19]

---

19   For examinations of the creation of the musical canon, see Citron, *Gender,* pp. 2-14.

Chapter 1
Court as Theater and Theater at Court

Theatricality is a linchpin of the Baroque aesthetic. In this theater that is their lives, the nobility, especially those at the highest rungs of the aristocracy, are always on display. Their private lives could never be completely divorced from the public's need for a good show.

Consider that one of the purposes of pomp and circumstance is to inspire and awaken a sense of awe in people. The private cultural productions of the nobility found their way into the public realm: first through newspaper reports about their activities, and later through publication of these creative endeavors. Life for the nobility could be described as a series of theatrical events—public appearances at the trade fairs, visits to smaller courts throughout the realm, state dinners concluding with an evening of entertainment in the private quarters, which included dancing and music-making on the part of nobles and professionals.

Music-Historical Contexts in Munich and Dresden

Maria Antonia's creativity can best be understood through knowledge of some of the history of her family, their relation to society, and the nobility's interactions with members of other classes, especially with musicians, poets, and writers.

Munich was the seat of the dukes of Upper Bavaria (from the house of Wittelsbach) from 1255 and became the capital of the duchy in 1550. Musical connections of German-speaking musicians with the imperial court date back to the 15th century, with Ludwig Senfl's appointment. He had previously sung in and directed the Kantorei of the court chapel for Emperor Maximilian I. This Kantorei performed for both secular and sacred functions.

From the time of Orlando Lassus' appointment as Hofkapellmeister in 1563, music took on a decidedly Italian flavor, as the internationally educated Lassus directed an ensemble which recruited increasingly more Italians. Andrea and Giovanni Gabrieli were among those who played at court under Lassus.

With Duke Albrecht V (r. 1550-79) came Munich's reputation as a center of the arts, due to his enormous collection of music, paintings, and sculptures, which form the nucleus of the present-day Bavarian state art collections, library, and other institutions. With the Duke's invitation, the Jesuits came to Munich in 1559, and religious life in that city took on a new importance.

The Jesuits opened educational institutions for the poor and invited court musicians to teach music to their students. Jesuit plays produced at St. Michael's Church (consecrated 1597) drew audiences away from secular plays performed in the Rathaus and in town squares. The Jesuit order was seen at this time and had been known historically to be highly supportive of musical and dramatic performance by its adherents. The Thirty Years' War interrupted musical and cultural developments in

Bavaria and throughout the German states of the Empire. The court stayed Catholic following the Reformation.

Opera Comes to the Munich Court

Opera had its beginnings in Munich when the Elector Maximilian I (r. 1598-1651) converted a granary next to the Salvatorkirche into an opera house. His son Ferdinand Maria (Elector from 1651-1679) was a harpsichordist and was known to participate actively in opera productions at court. Ferdinand's spouse, Henriette Adelheid of Savoy (1636-1676), was a singer, harpist, and guitarist, and historians consider her to be the true driving force behind increased musical activity at court.[20] Italian operas began to be performed regularly, and from 1656 on, the lavish productions in Munich rivaled any in Europe.

It was from this time, as well, that the Hofkapellmeister was placed in charge of both secular and sacred productions. French music came briefly to the court under Elector Maximilian II Emanuel (r. 1679-1726), during his appointment as governor of the Netherlands during the War of the Spanish Succession (1701-14). As a child, he had received musical instruction from Hofkapellmeister Johann Kaspar Kerll, and was musically active as a player of the bass viol. His chamber musicians led by Pietro Torri and later by E. F. Dall'Abaco were brought by the Elector to Brussels and with him again during his exile in France. When the Elector returned to Munich in 1715, he brought French musicians to the court.

For the betterment of his son and future elector Karl Albrecht, however, an emphasis was placed on Italian culture. The Prince's journey through Italy lasted one year, from 1715 to 1716 and upon his return, Italian music began a resurgence at the court of Munich.

---

20 See *New Grove*, "Munich".

Karl Albrecht now personally oversaw the opera productions, a task to which his father had attended.[21]

Maria Antonia's World

Italian culture and classical literature would be the musical environment of Maria Antonia's childhood. In 1722, Tomaso Albinoni was invited to Munich to conduct his operas *I veri amici* and *Il trionfo dell'amore* for the wedding celebration of Karl Albrecht and Maria Amalia.[22] The Italian Baroque splendor of Nymphenburg and of portions of the Residenzschloss in Munich are partially Karl Albrecht's doing. Each is elaborately decorated with scenes from classical mythology and with musical motifs. Karl Albrecht's interests included the writing of Italian-language poetry, some of which were set to music by his court composer, Giovanni Ferrandini.[23] In her youth, Maria Amalia had participated in music-making at the imperial family's gatherings, singing elaborate cantatas by their court composer Giuseppe Porsile.[24]

Maria Antonia was born into this environment in 1724. Her education consisted of those subjects necessary to her roles as daughter, Duchess (and later Princess), wife, Electress, and—it would be hoped—Queen. Therefore, Latin, French (the lingua franca of all the aristocracy which had the ability to set them apart and which created a common culture among a certain class), mathematics, science, music, and literature were all part of her instruction. From her mother and

---

21 *Max II Emanuel,* p. 301.
22 Sets were designed by Giuseppe Galli Bibiena, who would later create sets for Maria Antonia's operatic productions.
23 Letter from Wackerbarth to Brühl, 6 Nov 1748.
24 She was also an avid rider and hunter. Karl Albrecht had the Amalienburg hunting lodge at Nymphenburg specially built for Maria Amalia.

father came a love of Italian music and culture.[25] Her siblings also received this same education in music and liberal arts.[26] Maximilian III Joseph played the bass viol, as his grandfather had done, and was also noted in his lifetime as a composer.[27] All the sisters played harpsichord, but Maria Josepha was thought the best harpsichordist in the family. Maria Antonia was known as a singer, and she had access to some of the finest musicians at her parent's court for her composition and singing teachers, including Giovanni Ferrandini and Giovanni Porta. Her vocal ability by the age of 16 was proficient enough to allow her to perform the lead female role in a pastoral given for her grandmother, the Empress Dowager, in Vienna.

With his inheritance of the electorship in 1726, Karl Albrecht appointed Torri as Kapellmeister, who served from 1732-37, and Italian music dominated the court once again. Torri was succeeded by Giovanni Porta (Hofkapellmeister 1737-55). Warfare disrupted Maria Antonia's youth when her father provoked the War of the Austrian Succession (1740-45) by contesting Maria Theresia's right to inherit the imperial throne, and the Bavarian monarch, along with his family, was forced to flee Munich. Some musicians from court went with the family into exile, including Giovanni Ferrandini.

Karl Albrecht had himself elected Emperor and crowned as such in Frankfurt. Having accomplished this goal, he was unable to return to

---

25 Maria Antonia also inherited their passion for hunting. She participated in the hunts in Munich, and she is portrayed, along with her mother, father, and brother Maximilian III Joseph, in the paintings of the hunts which can be found in Amalienburg. Interestingly, the current descriptions of the paintings mention her brother, but not Maria Antonia, who is clearly depicted. Thus continues the erasure of women's histories. In Dresden, she is the only Saxon Princess to have earned the distinction of having had hunting pistols made specially for her. See Schaal, "Die Leibwaffen der Kurfürstin Maria Antonia. Aus dem Historischen Museum, Dresden."

26 They were Theresia Benedicta Maria (1725-1743), Maximilian III Joseph (1727-1777), Maria Anna Josepha (1734-1776), and Josepha Maria (1739-1767).

27 Maximilian III Joseph took after his sister in composing music for chamber groups. His music survives in Dresden, in contemporary scores copied by Pisendel as well as in prints. All of his music seems to be housed in Dresden, leading me to believe that Maria Antonia inherited it upon her brother's death in 1777.

Munich to reign for two years due to its having been invaded by Maria Theresia's troops. Only when a peace was reached was he finally able to return to Munich in 1745, though his land had been ravaged by war. He died shortly thereafter.[28]

Although Maria Antonia was the eldest child, being female, she could not become Elector. Therefore, upon Karl Albrecht's death, Maria Antonia's brother Maximilian III Joseph inherited the title of Elector of Bavaria, forswore any claims on imperial power, and set about restoring Bavaria to financial and political health.[29] At just this time, the court of Dresden became interested in strengthening its economic and political ties to other European dynasties. Maria Amalia, the Dowager Empress, now saw the need to arrange marriages for her eldest daughter, Maria Antonia, and her only son, Maximilian III Joseph.

The recent marriage of Maria Josepha (daughter to Friedrich August II and Maria Josepha, daughter of Holy Roman Emperor Joseph I) to the Dauphin gave Saxony a powerful ally in the French court. Later in 1747, the double wedding of Maria Anna and Friedrich Christian of Saxony to Maximilian III Joseph and Maria Antonia, respectively, strengthened the blood ties of the Saxon royal electoral family to the Holy Roman Empire and cemented political ties between Saxony and Bavaria. The role of music in the civic and court life in Dresden would also have played a part in considering its suitability for the Bavarian electoral family.

---

28 He died in 1745. That same year Maria Theresia's spouse, Franz Stephan, was elected Emperor under the name Franz I. Maria Theresia ruled through her husband since she was the direct descendant of the emperor. This is a fascinating study in gender and power in its own right.

29 Max III Joseph completed the opera house begun by his father, the Cuvilliéstheater, in 1753, and appointed Bernasconi as Hofkapellmeister (1755-84). He continued to commission works by Italian composers, but increasingly German composers began to receive his patronage, among them Johann Naumann from Dresden, a protege of Maria Antonia's.

The Music of the Dresden Court

Dresden was one of the many towns in Saxony which the Wettins founded in order to consolidate their power in the 13th century. It became the seat of the Albertine branch of the Wettin family in the late 15th century. The family's participation in the musical life of the city can be traced back to Margrave Heinrich der Erlauchte (r. 1227-88) who was a minstrel.[30] Sacred and secular music at court began to achieve prominence after the Reformation. The earliest permanent body of musicians at court is thought to have been a band of wind players, and the dukes, later electors, maintained bands of trumpeters and a timpanist for both musical and military usage.

A Hofkantorei consisting of singers and instrumentalists was founded in 1548 and led by Johann Walter, a singer and composer appointed its first Hofkapellmeister. Netherlandish music was at the core of their repertoire, although Italian musicians and works were gradually introduced. Heinrich Schütz (1585-1672) was appointed Kapellmeister in 1617, but the outbreak of the Thirty Years' War reduced his Kapell to just a handful of players by the mid-1630s. Much of his time between 1633 and 1645 was spent visiting other courts.

Italian influence continued to grow, with the Elector Johann Georg II (r. 1665-80) hiring many Italian musicians. Although the musicians at court continued to be a mix of nationalities—German, Italian, and Bohemian—with the conversion of Elector Friedrich August to Catholicism in 1697, French musicians and culture came to dominate court life.

What is referred to by historians as the "Golden Age" of music at the Dresden court began with ascension to the throne of the Elector Friedrich August I (called August the Strong) in 1694. His 1697 conversion to Catholicism allowed him to become elected King of Poland (as August

---

30 Six of his songs are to be found in the Heidelberg Manesse manuscript. See *New Grove*, "Dresden."

II). Soon after his conversion, he reorganized the Hofkapelle into the Evangelische Hofkirchenmusik and the Churfürstliche (or Königliche) Sächsische Capell- und Cammer-Musique. The musicians were highly qualified, and most specialized in a single instrument. Violin, viola, cello, and double bass were represented, as were wind instruments such as the transverse flute, oboe, bassoon, and horn, and continuo instruments including lutes, pantaleon, harpsichord, and organ. Court trumpeters and drummers were an ensemble unto themselves but played with the Hofkapelle when required. The King-Elector's tastes ran to all things French in music, art, and lifestyle, including various mistresses, in apparent emulation of Louis XIV. French singers, musicians, and dancers make up a large proportion of the Capell- und Cammer-Musique roster from these years.

The change from French to Italian influences on life at the court of Dresden follows a chronology similar to that of Munich. Perhaps in both cases, it stems in part from a growing political shift, following the death of Louis XIV in 1715, towards closer musical and cultural ties within the Holy Roman Empire.[31] Twelve musicians and artists moved within a circle that linked Dresden to Munich (to Prague) and to Vienna. And as the Elector Maximilian II Emanuel had done, when it came time for the Elector to send his successor on a voyage of discovery and education, the Italian peninsula was the destination of choice.

The Electoral Prince brought many court musicians with him on his journey, including Johann Georg Pisendel (1687-1755). Pisendel had been trained by Torelli and had studied with Vivaldi during the Crown Prince's Grand Tour of 1716-17. When Pisendel became Konzertmeister, the music at court leaned distinctly towards things Italian, and when Friedrich August II returned to court in 1717, it was as an admirer of Italian music and culture. During his Grand Tour, the

---

31 The use of marriage to cement political alliances with the imperial family is also a note-worthy aspect of this trend.

Electoral Prince engaged Italian instrumentalists and singers to form an Italian opera company in Dresden. Three operas of Antonio Lotti, *Giove in Argo*, *Ascanio,* and *Teofane* were performed for the wedding festivities of the prince to Maria Josepha.

An opera scandal, as the story is often told, erupted when too little money collided with too many egos after the wedding. Shortly after the festivities, the opera company broke up, and the best singers were hired away by Handel for his London company. Most of the Italian instrumentalists, including such luminaries as Francesco Maria Veracini also took their leave of Dresden, and the opera house was closed and reorganized. The opera reopened in 1726 with a new company; Johann Adolf Hasse and his spouse, the internationally famous soprano Faustina Bordoni were hired to the Cammer-Musique (as Hofkapellmeister and Prima Donna) after Friedrich August II's accession to the throne in 1734. Hasse's *opere serie* were given lavish productions both in Dresden, and at the court's other palaces such as Hubertusburg (near Dresden) and in Warsaw, Poland. The Elector's birthday, 7 October, was always an occasion for an opera production at Hubertusburg.

Friedrich August II gave all of his children an education which included music.[32] Prince Carl was a flutist, Princesses Elisabeth and Cunigunde were singers, and Elisabeth further distinguished herself as a dancer and harpsichordist.

The year 1740 brought with it a journey by the Electoral Prince Friedrich Christian to Italy. He was concerted by Antonio Vivaldi and brought many works by Vivaldi and others home to Dresden. Friedrich Christian was also inducted into the Arcadian Academy at this time and given the name "Lusazio Arigrero."[33] A 1746 visit of the Prince to Munich brought him into contact with Maria Antonia for the

---

32　The German nobility of the 18th century seem to have possessed a musicality unusual for the time. The broader social implications of this have yet to be studied.
33　See Giorgetti Vichi, *Gli Arcadi dal 1690 al 1800.* p. 171.

first time. A passionate correspondence ensued, and a lavish double wedding was arranged: Friedrich Christian of Saxony and Poland to Maria Antonia of Bavaria and Maximilian III Joseph of Bavaria to Maria Anna of Saxony and Poland.

Maria Antonia's life in the public eye begins with her marriage in June 1747. It was a double wedding for the houses of Wettin (Saxony) and Wittelsbach (Bavaria). Since the kingly family[34] covered the costs, it was an enormous affair. The events lasted for nearly half a month and were held, for the most part, in Dresden. Maximilian III Joseph married by proxy, and Maria Anna traveled to Munich after the formalities took place. Maria Antonia traveled from Munich.

For the festivities, operas were commissioned, gala feasts took place, silver coins bearing the images of the betrothed and commemorating the union were minted and thrown to the populace from castle windows, and even the royal porcelain factory in Meissen produced special figurines portraying Maria Antonia and Friedrich Christian as the idealized lovers of a gallant Arcadian drama. A document entitled *Concordia Pax et Amor* was published by the royal press, lauding the happy couples in Latin prose. A fireworks display at the palace at Pillnitz culminated the month's events and could be seen for miles around. Hasse and Pasquini's *La spartana generosa ovvero Archidamia* was composed specially for the occasion.

---

34 The Elector of Saxony was also the elected King in Poland at this time.

Chapter 2
The Princess' Musical Influences

Maria Antonia's music catalog is the best evidence we have for her musical education. It reads like a Who's Who of 18th-century Italian opera. If one looks at aria count alone, it would seem that Hasse was her favorite composer since his works outnumber those of others. However, his works only begin to appear in large numbers in the portions of the catalog that were written in Dresden. I therefore posit that he was a later influence in her musical life, not an early one. In her formative years, the Princess collected works by a variety of composers, with the works of Jomelli, Ferrandini, and Manna being of interest to her. The catalog shows that Maria Antonia gleaned a musical education not only through formal composition lessons, but also through the performance of this music.

When Maria Antonia married Friedrich Christian of Saxony and Poland, she brought with her a treasure trove of music, to which she continued to add. Entitled *Catalogo de[i] Libri Numerati Musicali D: S: A: R: M: A: D: de B.* (De Son Altesse Royale Maria Antonia Dux de Bavaria), it appears to date from after 1746. It is bound in red leather, and measures 9" x 12". It is, in part, a listing of individual arias and complete operatic scores (see Illustration 2.1).

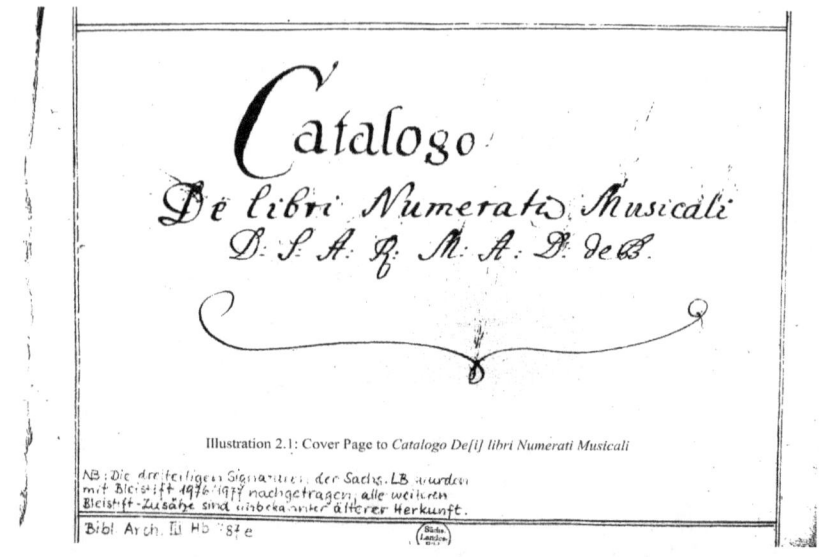

Illustration 2.1: Cover Page to *Catalogo De[i] libri Numerati Musicali*

Most of these scores are still extant, and the catalog has pencil markings from 20th-century librarians listing present-day call numbers. There exist pencil marks of uncertain historical origin as well. The catalog is divided into two parts: the first with incipits and the second merely a listing of titles.

The following table is my transcription of the first part of the music catalog:

Table 2.1: Catalogo de[i] Libri Numerati Musicali

Composer	Types of works	Location in Catalog	Total Arias
Abaco	Arias: "Ein Buch mit blauen samet eingebunden [sic]"	p.72	
Abos [spelled Abbos]	Arias	pp. 24-25, 27, 33-35	9

Table 2.1: Catalogo de[i] Libri Numerati Musicali

Composer	Types of works	Location in Catalog	Total Arias
Albertis	Arias	pp. 27, 37	2
Battoni	Arias	pp. 17-19, 27	14
Bernasconi	Arias	pp. 19, 34, 37-41, 48	7
Bertoni	Arias	pp. 20, 25, 34	4
Carnaci	Arias	p. 67	2
Chiarino	Arias	p.78	1
Cocchi	Arias	pp. 12, 100	6
Conti	Arias	p. 14	2
Ferrandini	Arias, Cantatas, Operas	pp. 3, 8, 56-57, 85, 90-91	24+
Galuppi	Arias	pp. 32-33, 39	6
Giaÿ	Arias	p. 15	2
Gluck	Arias	p. 14	2
Graun	Arias	p. 79	6
Hasse	Arias, Operas	pp. 9-10, 13, 20, 28-29, 30-31, 36-38, 46-47, 49-63, 69, 73-84, 86-89, 92-96	240+
Terradellas	Arias	pp. 11, 33-34, 36	12
Verracini (sic)	Duettini	pp. 43-44	12
Vicentino	Arias	p. 66	1
Vinci	Opera Artaserse	p. 70	
Wagenseil	Arias	pp. 20, 25	2
"Composte da N"	"Arie sei mit 4 safran buecher"	p. 68	6
N	Arias	pp. 15-17, 19, 21, 23, 32, 35-36, 39, 47, 66-67	22

Table 2.1: Catalogo de[i] Libri Numerati Musicali

Composer	Types of works	Location in Catalog	Total Arias
No author listed	"Arien mit 4 Rothe [rote] buecher;" "Ein francoisses [sic] buech mit francoishe [sic] Arien"	p. 71	

There are three sets of scribal hands in this first part (see Illustration 2.2), the first hand having entered the information from pages 1-79 (or books I to XXXXV), the second hand appearing from pages 80-96 (books XXXXVI to LI) and the third from pages 97-100 (books 52 and 53; note the change from Roman to Arabic numerals).

Illustration 2.2a: Scribal Hand A

Illustration 2.2b: Scribal Hand B

Illustration 2.2c: Scribal Hand C

Pages 100-126 are blank. This part of the catalog is annotated with incipits. A clue to the origin of at least Scribe A is the numeral 8 in time signatures. As written in the first part of the catalog, the 8 is written on its side, much like an infinity sign. This appears only in manuscripts from the Munich court (see Illustration 2.3).

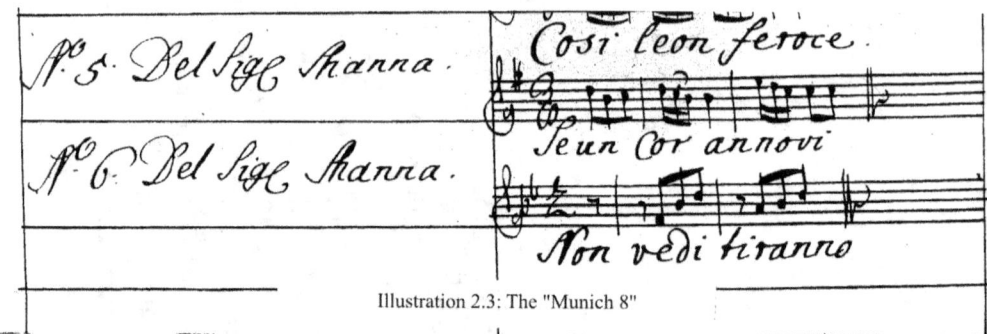

Illustration 2.3: The "Munich 8"

The third scribal hand also wrote the second part of the catalog, whose title page reads: *Catalogo. / Dei Libri di Musica con I numeri negri. / La prima colonna significa i numeri / dei Libri. / La Seconda gli Autori./La Terza i Titoli dei Libri / La Quarta la quantità de i [sic] Libri conte, / nuti sotto l'istesso numero.*[35] This second part of the catalog does not duplicate material found in the first part. It is organized by composer, although not alphabetically:

Table 2.2: Catalogo Dei Libri di Musica con i numeri negri

No.	Composer	Title	Vols.
1	Hasse	La Conversione di Sant' Agostino	1
2	Hasse	L'Antigono	1
3	Hasse	Didone abbandonata	1
4	Hasse	Arie	1
5	Hasse	Cantata per li 3. d'Agosto	1
6	Hasse	Cantata per li 8. Di Dicembre	1
7	Hasse	Ipermestra	3

---

35 Catalog./ of the Music Books with black numerals./The first column indicates the numbers of the Books./The Second the Authors./The Third the Titles of the Books./The Fourth the quantity of the Books contained under the same number.

Table 2.2: Catalogo Dei Libri di Musica con i numeri negri

No.	Composer	Title	Vols.
8	Hasse	Dodeci Arie	1
9	Hasse	Il Natal di Giove	1
10	Hasse	Atilio Regolo	3
11	Hasse	Archidamia	3
12	Hasse	Lucio Papirio	3
13	Hasse	Demofoonte	3
14	Hasse	Leucippo	3
15	Hasse	Il Ciro riconosciuto	3
16	Hasse	Adriano	3
17	Ferrandini	Opera Francese	3
18	Ferrandini	Cantata à Voce Sola	1
19	Ferrandini	Cantate	1
20	Ferrandini	Ariette à Voce sola	1
21	Ferrandini	Cantata da Camera a Voce Sola, e Basso	1
22	Ferrandini	Cantata à Voce Sola e stromenti	1
23	Porpora	Statira	1
24	Porpora	La Semiramide	3
25	Porpora	La Camilla	3
26	Porpora	Filandro	1
27	Porpora	Oronte e Climene	
28	Ristori	Semiramide	3
29	Ristori	I Lamenti d'Orfeo	1
30	Ristori	Didone abbandonata Cantata	1
31	Ristori	Lavinia a Turno	1
32	Ristori	Nice a Tirsi	1
33	Leonardo Leo	Sant Elena	1
34	Leonardo Leo	La Morte d'Abelle	1
35	Pergolesi	La Serva Padrona	1
36	Pergolesi	IV. Cantate	1
37	Pergolesi	XI. Arie	1
38	Pergolesi	XI. Arie	1

Table 2.2: Catalogo Dei Libri di Musica con i numeri negri

No.	Composer	Title	Vols.
39	Baldas: Galuppi	Gustavo Primo Re di Suezia	1
40	Baldas: Galuppi	Artaserse	3
41	Porta	Il Gianguir.	3
42	Porta	Il Farnace	3
43	Porta	Ifegenia	3
44	Giuseppe Scarlatti	Amor Prigioniero.	1
45	Cavalier Scarlatti	Oratorio à 3 Voci.	
46	Giuseppe Carnaci	Serenata	1
47		La Concordia del Tempo colla Fama	1
48	Donna Maria Agnesi	Arie con Stromenti	1
49	Francesco Peli	La Clemenza di Tito	3
50	Angelo Somelli	Cantata à 3 Voci per la Notte del SS: Natale	1
51	Gio: Antonio Giaj	Adriano in Siria	1
52	Bernard: Albrandi	Mitridate.	3
53	Gennaro d'Alessandro	Adelaide	1
54	Jomelli	Didone	3
55	Giuseppe Bonno	Il Re Pastore	3
56	Gluck	Ezio	3
57	Rutini	Arie	1
58	Rutini	La Semiramide	1
59	P. Michele Breünich	Il David Penitente	1
60	Giuseppe Umstatt	Il Palladio conservato	1
61	Girolamo Abos	VIII. Arie	1
62	Schürer	La Galatea	1
63	Schürer	Cantata per li 18 di Luglio	1
64	Schürer	Astrea placata	
65	Schürer	Doris Teutsch [sic]	
66	Schürer	L'Ercole sul Termodonte	
67	Carlo Enrico Graun	Opera Cinna	3
68		Ifigenia in Aulide	

Table 2.2: Catalogo Dei Libri di Musica con i numeri negri

No.	Composer	Title	Vols.
69	Rameau	Platée Comedic-Ballet	1
70	Rameau	Les Festes de l'Hymen et de l'Amour	1
71	Rameau	Les Indes Galantes. Ballet.	1
72	Pietro Grua	Duetti da Camera	1
73	Giuseppe Orlandini	Cantate VI Todesche [sic], et un Intermezzo Serpilla e Bacocco	1
74	N:	Cantate Francesi	2
75	N:	Arie diverse	1
76	N:	Intermezi [sic] Comichi	1
77	N:	Pastorale	1
78	Porta	Gianguir	3
79	Marcello, Bononcini, Albinoni, et altri	Cantate	1
80	N:	Motet Spirituell per Chiesa	1
81	N:	Cantate	1
82	N:	Meditazione 1ma e 2da del Anno 1746	4
83	N:	La Semiramide	2
84	N:	Arie di Tito	1
85	N:	Comoedia Frisingana	1
86	Porta	Farnace Atto II. e III. NB: manco il Primo.	2
87	Porta	Ifigenia	2
88	N:	Oratorio Abramo	1
89	N:	Arie diverse	1
90	Caballone, Araÿa, Jacomelli, et altri	Arie diverse	1
91	N:	Der Vertauschte Arsaces	3
92	N:	La Nascita d'Amalia	1
93	N:	Giove Fulminator de Giganti	1

Table 2.2: Catalogo Dei Libri di Musica con i numeri negri

No.	Composer	Title	Vols.
94	Hasse, Pergolesi, Pulli, Leo, Bernasconi, et altri	XIV. Duetti	1
95	Hasse, Pepe de Majo, Perez, Jomelli	VIII. Arie	1
96	Caldera, et altri.	Canoni à 3. E 4.	1
97	Chiarini, Carcani, Barba, Galuppi	Arie	1
98	N:	Pastorale Todesca [sic]	1
99	Caballone, Sarri, Hasse, Vinci, Porpora, etaltri.	Arie. Canto e Basso	1
100	Albrandi	Stabat Mater	1
101	N:	Cantata nel Giorno di Nascita di Cristiano Federico P. E. di S:	1
102	N:	Irene	1
103	N:	Duo in Dialogue	1
104	N:	XII. Arie	1
105	N:	Cantata Teutsch	1
106	Antonius Paganelli	Odæ Sex Selectæ	1
107	N:	Nicomede	1
108	Abate Stefano	Duetti.	1
109	Nicolo Porpora	Sinfonie da Camera à tre	3
110	Antonio Bonporti	Concerti à quattro.	4
111	Antonio Vivaldi	Concerti con molti Istromenti	1
112	Teofilo Muffat	Componimenti Musicali per il Cembalo	1
113	Wenceslao Wodiczka	Sei Sonate à Violino Solo, e Basso	1
114	Wenceslao Wodiczka	Huit Sonates pour le Violon et la Basse	1
115	Wenceslao Wodiczka	Sei Sonate à Violino Solo, e Basso	1

Table 2.2: Catalogo Dei Libri di Musica con i numeri negri

No.	Composer	Title	Vols.
116	Gio: Gioacchino Quantz	Sei Sonate à Flauto Traversiere Solo, e Cembalo	1
117	Binder	Sei Sonate per il Cembalo.	1
118	Joseph de Paur	Six Sonates pour le Violon et la Basse.	1
119	N:	Receuil de Contredanses	1
120	Egidio Lasnel	La Conversione di Sant Agostino	

Pages 135-140 are empty. Pencil markings that indicate that this was a catalog in progress. For example, "Mandate a Monaco" (Sent to Munich) recurs throughout, showing an active exchange of material between Maria Antonia and her brother Maximilian III Joseph. The titles of some works at the end of the catalog are written in pencil, a further indication that this was not a finished document.

Further analysis of the catalog reveals a knowledge of Italian opera from the early to late 1700s. Scribe A's portion of the catalog contains arias by Jomelli (book I), Ferrandini (books II, V), Manna (books III and IV), Hasse (books VI, VIII), Terradellas (book VII), Cocchi (book VII), Battoni (book X), Abos (book XIII) among others. In addition to it being the largest section of her catalog, there is a greater variety of composers in this part of the book than in the others. Scribe B's portion contains only arias by Hasse (drawn from his operas *Alfonso, Senocrita* and *Cleofide)* and operas by Ferrandini (*Artaxerse*, book XXXXVII, *Pastorale* book XXXXIX, and *Adriano* book L). Scribe C's portion contains only arias by Rinaldo di Capua and David Perez (book 52) and Jomelli and Cocchi (book 53).

The second part of the catalog, "the books with the black numerals," consists in large part of scores in manuscript. Some apparently came with her from Munich as evidenced by their format and by Maria Antonia's coat of arms on the cover. The acquisition of others dates from after Maria Antonia's arrival in Dresden. Some of the works listed are those for which she provided the texts (cantatas set by Ristori, the oratorio *La conversione di Sant'Agostino* set by both Hasse and Lasnel, and some of the secular works set by Ferrandini). Most of the Hasse operas listed here were premiered in Dresden or Hubertusburg.[36]

The composer "N" has created confusion for Maria Antonia's biographers, and so I hope to clarify matters somewhat here. Basing my findings upon annotations in the works by Fürstenau, the only works under "N" that are indeed music by Her Highness are the "Arie sei mit 4 safran buecher."[37] Most of the others for which doubtful attributions to Maria Antonia are ascribed contain her name written on their title page as a mark of ownership.

As music had been a daily part of her existence in Munich, so was it also in Dresden. The Italian opera performances at the opera house in the Zwinger and at prime minister Brühl's theater took place in the autumn and during carnival season, times when the King and Queen were in residence in Dresden. These were the most public forms of music-making since anyone suitably dressed could obtain free entry to the performances.

For the royal family's private enjoyment of music, chamber music was prized. This included not only instrumental music for variously sized ensembles, but also vocal music ranging from solo cantatas to chamber operas. Many of these performances took place in the Taschenbergpalais, the princely palace located directly behind the Residenzschloss in Dresden. Others took place at the smaller palaces

---

36 For more detailed information on first performances, see the *New Grove* articles on the respective composers.

37 See also Petzholdt, *Maria Antonia Walpurgis. Kurfurstin von Sachsen, Geb. Prinzessin von Bayern.*

belonging to the royal family that lay just outside the 18th-century city's walls: the palaces in the Türkischer Garten and the Grosser Garten, in Übigau, in Hubertusburg, and in Großsedlitz among several.

These performances involved members of the royal family as well as invited professionals, both singers and instrumentalists. Name days, wedding anniversaries, saint's days, death remembrances, and birthdays marked occasions for a combination of public and private celebrations and were the main rituals that marked the life of the royal family, and therefore of the other members of the court.

For the birthdays of the King and Queen in 1747, Maria Antonia premiered cantatas she wrote for them: *Grande Augusto* and *Che ti dirò, Regina?*, both set to music by their Majesties' favorite composer, Hasse. The performance for the King took place on his name day, August 3, and that for the Queen took place on her birthday, December 8. Her cantatas were warmly received.

Chapter 3

Maria Antonia's Artistry
Gains Recognition

Graf Wackerbarth-Salmour was Friedrich Christian's Privy Councillor, and part of his duty was to inform the Prime Minister (and therefore the King and Queen) of the happenings at Dresden when the King was in Warsaw. These letters provide a unique account of the daily musical lives of the court. It was not only the royal family that participated in music making, but also professional musicians and "l'affluence de Dames de la Cour et de la Ville."[38] On another occasion, "Madame the Royal and Electoral Princess sang. . . With la <u>Rosa</u> the adjoining <u>Cantata</u>. The music is by the famous <u>Manna</u> and the words are from an anonymous pen. All the Ladies and Cavaliers, not to mention the Priest and the Minister of England who had the honor to hear this <u>Cantata</u> were ravished and enchanted."[39]

---

38 Wackerbarth letter, 20 Juillet 1748, referring to events of Maria Antonia's birthday celebration.
39 Wackerbarth letter, 21 Decembre 1748: "Madame la Princesse Roïale Elect:ᴵᵉ chanta. . . Avec la <u>Rosa</u> la <u>Cantata</u> ci-jointe. La Musique est du fameux <u>Manna</u> et les paroles sont d'une plume annonime. Toutes les Dames et Cavaliers, sans oublier le Nonce et le Ministre d'Angleterre, qui ont eu l'honneur d'entendre cette <u>Cantata</u> en ont été ravis et enchantés."

Maria Antonia's creative output increased from the moment she set foot in the Taschenbergpalais. Her first works from this period were translations into French of a "Miserere," first sent discreetly in manuscript to various acquaintances, and then published under a pseudonym. Her production of poetry increased, and she continued the practice begun in Munich of setting her texts to music. She wrote both French and Italian language poetry and set all of these texts in the Italian manner. In 1748, Maria Antonia was inducted into Rome's prestigious Arcadian Academy, which had as its goal the reform of Italian poetry (the imperial court poet Pietro Metastasio was a member of this group).[40] Documents in Latin and Greek commemorate this induction.

Another part of her duty was to give birth to an heir to the throne. During her first pregnancy, Maria Antonia continued to be active in performing music and engaging in other activities.[41] News of her pregnancy found its way into newspapers such as the Hamburg Gazette. Maria Antonia's earliest attempts to be actively involved in political matters aside from giving birth to the next Wettin seem to have met with some resistance: both the Prince and Princess were kept at arm's length from the running of the government.[42]

It seems at times that the Prime Minister and Privy Councillor hoped that musical activities would distract the attentions of the princely pair from political matters. In a letter from 27 Nov 1748, Wackerbarth describes compliments he gave to the Princess on her singing: "I had just said to Madame the Princess Royal that her presentation of her

---

40 She was the fourth member of the house of Wittelsbach to receive this honor. Her uncles Clemens August (as Etindo Aristerio) and Philip Moritz (as Italgo Ermioneo) had been inducted in 1717, and her cousin Clemens Franz (as Norisio/Noricio Aretuseo) was inducted in 1743. See *Gli Arcadi*, pp. 105, 150, and 194.

41 Wackerbarth to Brühl, 5 Juin 1748: "J'ai eû beau dire à Madame la Princesse R.:le qu'un juge competent a fait lecture de sa Cantata; qu'elle etoit une production digne de la grande et incomparable voix, qui en la recitant lui a donné encor plus de grace et de force etc."

42 See Schlechte, *Das geheime politische Tagebuch des Kurprinzen Friedrich Christian 1751 bis 1757*, and Wackerbarth to Brühl, 27 Nov 1748.

Cantata was considered favorably, that it was a production dignified for a large and incomparable voice, that the recitative had given it still more grace and power, etc." However, Maria Antonia is less interested in a compliment than in hearing about the actions of the Senate Council. Wackerbarth does not appear to have wished to divulge information: "...she always returned to the Senate Council. 'When will it finish?' She said to me. 'What action will they take?'"[43] He does not tell her anything she does not already know, and Maria Antonia is displeased.[44]

Since the Elector of Saxony was also King in Poland, the court was required to spend a portion of each year in Warsaw. This meant that the King and Queen, the Prime Minister, their retinues, and some musicians would remain for five or six months every year in Poland (usually January through March and again from May through July). A letter dated 5 June 1748 from Maria Josepha gives the Princess Royal the protocol for writing letters: They should be numbered, and they should always include a separate sheet upon which is inscribed "PS." The numbering system allowed them to determine whether their correspondence had gone astray. Rarely have the sheets with postscripts survived, but it is possible to assume that these postscripts were meant to carry politically sensitive information, and they were made to be detachable from the main letter and easily disposed of in a nearby fire.

After 1750, evidence of Maria Antonia's increasing involvement in the political goings-on of the court is found in her correspondence with the King and Queen. Several letters from after 1750 used disappearing ink, some of which is still legible.[45] Among these letters is a list of code names for each member of the family and for other members of the nobility.

---

43 Wackerbarth to Brühl, 5 Juin 1748: "...elle en est toûjours révenûe au Senatûs-Consilium. Quand finira-t-il? m'a-t-Elle dit. Quelle resolution y prendra-t on?"
44 Wackerbarth to Brühl, 27 Novembre 1748.
45 This applies equally to letters to and from Friedrich Christian.

Tragedy struck the young couple when Maria Antonia miscarried in 1749. This led the princely pair to travel to Prague to visit several Catholic shrines in September of that year.[46] They traveled incognito as the Comte et Comtesse de Lusace, staying at palaces of friends and relatives along the way. Music-making was part of the trip, especially during a surprise visit from her brother and his spouse.[47]

With her next pregnancy in early 1750, the Princess limited her involvement in musical and social activities. She spent much of her day reading and writing letters. Only when the pregnancy was well established did she take the occasional trip to the palace at Sedlitz or elsewhere. Mostly she kept to her chambers and listened to others concertize. She continued to write poetry, as evidenced by the production in April 1750 of *La conversione di Sant'Agostino,* Hasse's setting of her oratorio text, in the Hofkapelle. All of Maria Antonia's health precautions succeeded in the birth of Friedrich August on 23 Dec 1750, although his birth was not remarked upon in the *Hof-Calender*, and therefore not made public, until 1752. Maria Antonia eventually bore seven children, six of whom survived into adulthood. Two of them would become kings of Saxony.

It is first in 1751 that the public gets its official glimpse of the Princess Royal with the production of the regulation formal court portrait by the court painter Anton Raphael Mengs. It shows her in full royal regalia, crown at her side, wearing a pale blue court dress and the Austrian Order of the Star Cross and the Russian Order of Catherine (see it in the online collection of the Staatliche Kunstsammlungen

---

46 The documentation of this pilgrimage, entitled *Journal du Voyage, que LL AA RR^{les} Monseigneur le Prince et Madame la Princesse Electorale de Saxe ont fait à Prague sous le nome de Comte et Comtesse de Lusace au Mois de Septembre 1749* is contained in Loc. 3058 Vol III of the letters from Wackerbarth to Brühl.

47 And for those interested in ballroom etiquette, note that since Friedrich Christian was lame and could not walk unaided, and therefore could not dance, Maria Antonia opened a ball held during this stay with her brother: "Le souper fût précedé d'un Bal, dont Monseigneur l'Electeur et Mad^e la Princesse Electorale firent l'ouverture." From *Journal du Voyage.*

Dresden at this link: https://skd-online-collection.skd.museum/Details/Index/346810). This and the complementary portrait of her spouse (a pastel version which can be seen here: https://skd-online-collection.skd.museum/Details/Index/451170) are perfectly conventional.

Maria Antonia's portrait has more in common with those of earlier princesses of Saxony, Christine Eberhardine or Maria Josepha. These women were considered rocks of Christian piety from both sides of the religious spectrum: Christine Eberhardine was the first wife of August the Strong, and a staunch Lutheran; Maria Josepha was a thorough Catholic, daughter of Emperor Joseph I. This was a mantle that Maria Antonia would be expected to wear in her present role as Princess, and in her future role as Electress. What is unconventional is the accompanying portrait of their baby. This may be the first portrait of a royal child at such a young age—not even a year old.

These public portrayals belie the creative fire of these years. The next chapter will look at Maria Antonia's earliest works and at the settings of her Dresden poetry to music by the composers Hasse and Ristori.

Chapter 4

The Music and Poetry of
Maria Antonia's Youth

The sonic environment of Maria Antonia's youth would have included attendance at operas and church services in Munich at her grandfather's—later, her father's—court with music by Torri, Porta, and Ferrandini and at the imperial court of her maternal family where music by such composers as Porsile was popular. Of these, it was most likely Ferrandini who had the closest contact with the young Princess, and it is likely that he was her musical guide.

It is perhaps significant that the only musician from whom letters exist in Maria Antonia's collection are from or relating to Giovanni Ferrandini.[48] Ferrandini came to Munich as a boy. He was appointed to the Elector's court in 1723 as an oboist. From 1 April 1732, he was appointed chamber composer to the Elector. On 1 July 1737, he was made electoral advisor ("kurfürstlicher Rat") and director of chamber music. His operatic and instrumental works were performed in Munich, and some of his instrumental music was published in

---

48 D: Dla, Nachlässe 1 Nr 72, Briefe von und an Männer

Amsterdam. Pastorals by him were performed in Nymphenburg during Maria Antonia's childhood. Other works by him for the Bavarian court include operas on texts by Metastasio and Zeno.

During the War of the Austrian Succession, Ferrandini accompanied Karl Albrecht to Frankfurt and wrote a dramatic work for his coronation, the *Componimento drammatico per l'incoronazione di Carlo VII* in Frankfurt on 12 Feb 1742, now lost. The chamber composer would have been the one to instruct the young royals in musical matters.[49]

While little evidence remains to show what training the young Princess may have received, certainly she learned composition not just through formal written lessons (now lost), but through the transcription and performance of popular works. The best evidence for this comes from a book of twenty-nine arias, located in Dresden, long assumed to have been the work of Maria Antonia herself. In fact, it is a keyboard and voice reduction of the opera *Alessandro nell'Indie*, which was produced in the Munich court in 1735, and exists only in manuscript form.

Given the discoloration of the leather, and from its size and watermarks, the reduction appears to have originated in Munich and to date from before 1747. That it may have been a learning tool is clear from its incipit: Maria Antonia's name appears at the brackets to the opening system (see Illustration 4.1).

---

49 Sadie, Julie Anne, *Companion to Baroque Music*, p. 243

Illustration 4.1: Maria Antonia's Aria Book, Opening Page

This is not, as others have speculated, a mark of ownership, for in those scores that were simply part of her collection, the words "Maria Antonia Dux Bavariae" are written in a different ink by a different hand (see Illustration 4.2).

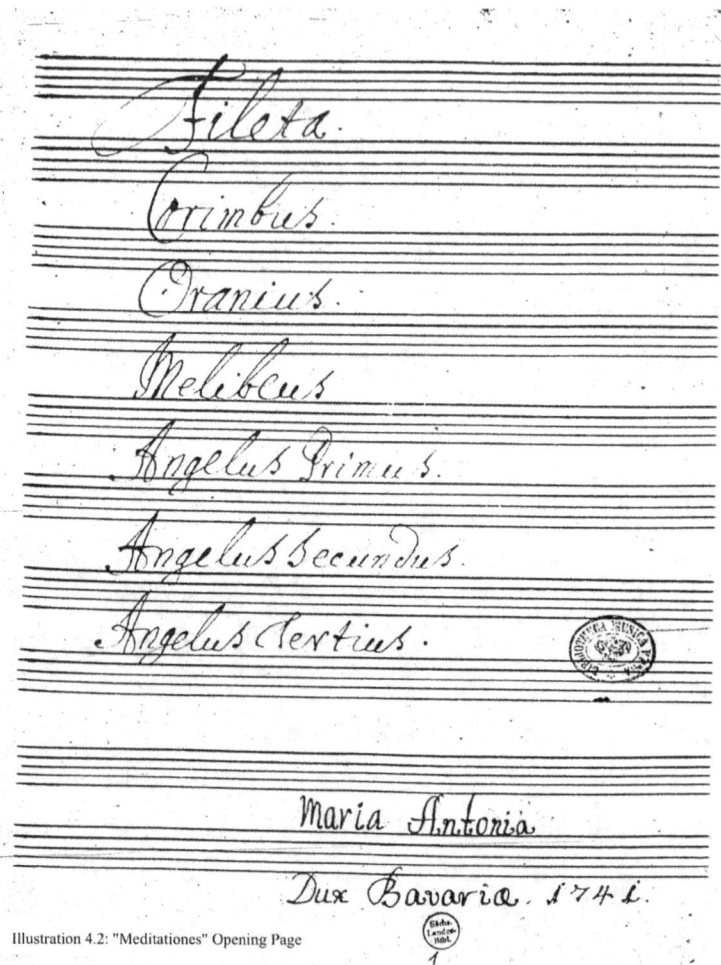

Illustration 4.2: "Meditationes" Opening Page

The writing of her name in Illustration 4.1 is much neater. The music is clearly not in her hand, but that of a scribe whose hand can be found in other scores originating in Munich. The collection shows signs of use, such as page tears, dog-ears on several pages, pencil markings, and wax drippings. Rather than being a mere record of the performance, this seems likely to have been used as an exercise in singing and accompanying oneself at the keyboard.

The earliest extant musical and literary composition from Maria Antonia herself is a set of six arias. It exists in two copies, both of which appear to have been copied by scribes from Munich, and therefore would have been among the works brought with Maria Antonia upon her marriage. They are listed in her 1747 catalog as "Arie sei mit 4 safran buecher." Here are the texts in the order given in D: Dlb Mus 3119-F-11, the score for these six arias:[50]

Aria allegro	*Aria allegro*
Perfido mi tradisti	Treacherous one you have betrayed me
e mi giurasti amore	and swore me love
e di vantarti hai core	and you have the nerve to boast
della tua fedeltà.	of your fidelity.
E mentre me rapisci	And while you take away
del cor l'interna pace	the peace from my heart
l'empio tuo cor fallace	your cruel and deceptive heart
ei pompa ancor me fa.	still boasts about itself.
Aria andante non presto	*Aria andante non presto*
Non parlarmi più d'amore	Don't speak to me any more of love
troppo è crudo il suo rigore.	too much is harsh in its severity.
Hò disciolta la catena,	I have undone the chain
e tornai in libertà.	and returned to freedom.
Ora sol ritorno in pace,	Only now I return in peace
che d'amor l'accesa face	since love's burning torch
più non tiene l'alma in pena	no longer holds the soul in pain
e più forza in me non hà.	and no longer has any power over me.

50 Text translations are my own. Accents in the Italian are in the original and have not been modernized.

Aria	*Aria*
Barbaro dispietato	Despicable barbarian
d'ogni mio ben mi privi	who deprives me of every good
perfido ancor vivi	treacherous one still you live
non ti punisce il ciel.	unpunished by the heavens.
Ma se del cielo irato	But if from an enraged heaven
il fulmini son lenti	the lightning flashes are slow
trema pur e ramenti	tremble and remember
ch'io vivo e son fedel.	that I live and am faithful.
Aria largo cantabile	*Aria largo cantabile*
Prendi l'ultimo addio	Take the last farewell
bell'idolo adorato	beautiful adored idol
più non chiamarmi ingrato	no longer call me ungrateful
ch'io moro à te fedel.	since I die faithful to you.
Rammentati ben mio	Remember my dear
che la ria morte stessa	that death itself
tien l'alma meno oppressa	holds the soul less oppressed
che un dubbio si crudel.	than a doubt so cruel.
Aria allegro moderato	*Aria allegro moderato*
Quanto è felice	How happy is
un cor costante	a constant heart
che dell'amante	that upon its beloved
fidarsi può.	can rely.

A me non lice	To me does not belong
questo contento,	this contentedness
per mio tormento	for my torment
ei m'inganno.	he deceived me.
Aria	*Aria*
Perdei l'amato bene	I lost my beloved
e l'alma è tanto oppressa,	and my soul is so oppressed,
che della morte istessa	that it implores from death itself
implora il rio favor.	the favor of dying.
Ah se le acerbe pene	Ah, if the harsh pains
non tolgano di vita	would not take my life
questa crudele aita	this cruel torment
di morte è ben peggior.	is worse than death.

Each aria expresses a different affect or emotion. *Perfido mi tradisti* and *Barbaro dispietato* are both rage arias, *Non parlarmi più d'amore* and *Quanto e felice* are both exercises in contrast/irony, and *Prendi l'ultimo addio* and *Perdei l'amato bene* are both laments. Three characters are thus delineated in six arias[51]. In the order presented above, the key schemes are G - A- F- G- A- F. However, the arias are listed on the cover page in the following order: *Prendi, Perfido, Quanto, Non parlarmi, Perdei,* and *Barbaro* which makes the key scheme G- G- A- A- F- F.[52] In some ways, the texts read like a cantata or chamber opera without the recitatives. In fact, there could be four characters depicted: the rage

---

51 This is made clearer by the ordering of the arias in D: Dlb Mus 3119-F-10, where the grouping is rage arias, contrast arias, and lament arias.
52 This order was taken by Fürstenau from a collection of Maria Antonia's poetry that no longer exists.

arias seem to be one character, the laments another, and the ironic ones could each be sung by two different characters.[53]

These arias are a study in text setting. As one would expect from a pedagogical standpoint, the student first learns to write poetry that is relatively simple and which expresses one or two clear ideas. The secular cantata, along with the *canzone* and *scenetto* were considered lighter forms, not necessarily requiring great character delineation. They are therefore ideal for a young poet/composer/singer.

These arias are for string orchestra, continuo, and soprano. The arias that share keys also share chord progressions; for example, both arias in A move from the relative minor at the start of the B section to its dominant; both arias in G move from parallel minor at the B section to the relative minor; both in F move from the relative minor to its dominant.

More interesting is the treatment of motifs between arias that share affects. For example, *Perfido* and *Barbaro* share a similar opening motive of a descending leap of a fifth followed by descending motion within an octave (see their opening statements in Illustrations 4.3a and 4.4a).

---

53 I would call the ironic ones "ambivalence arias," a term which I am perhaps coining to define compositions whose words say one thing but whose music implies the opposite emotion.

Illustration 4.3a: *Perfido, mi tradisti*, mm 12-23

Illustration 4.4a: *Barbaro dispietato*, mm 12-22

Both are in *alla breve*. In both, one notes the use of varied musical devices to express the text. In *Perfido*, for example, emphasis is placed on certain words through the use of melismas (Illustration 4.3b: "vantarti," boasting, at mm. 34-38) or long note values (Illustration 4.3b: "fedeltà," fidelity, at mm. 37-41), for example. *Perfido* further illustrates the text through use of the time signature change in m. 70 (Illus. 4.3c), which corresponds with the idea of seduction introduced in the first line of the second quatrain ("rapisci"). It shifts to a dance-like triple meter, and by the last two lines of the quatrain, the dance has become rather sinister when the music quickens to *presto* from *allegro*. *Barbaro* shares *Perfido*'s love of dazzling leaps and descending triplet figures. *Barbaro* builds excitement by using descending sixteenth-note runs (Illus. 4.4b: on "ciel" in voice mm. 23-32, later echoed by the violins, see Illus 4.4c).

Illustration 4.3b: *Perfido*, mm 34-41, "vantarti" and "fedeltà"

Illustration 4.3c: *Perfido*, mm 68-80

Illustration 4.4b: *Barbaro*, "mm 23-32, "ciel"

Illustration 4.4c: *Barbaro*, mm 33-41, "ciel" in violins

The contrast arias *Quanto è felice* and *Non parlarmi* use the same key to different ends. While both set the A section to A major, and the B section to F# minor, *Quanto* is direct in its handling of the text. It is in a dancing 3/8 throughout (Illustration 4.5a), which deceives the listener into thinking that the entire song will be cheerful.

Illustration 4.5a: *Quanto è felice*, mm 13-27

This makes the darker text of the B section (Illustration 4.5b, from m. 90) more striking. The B section speaks the truth, for the speaker of the first quatrain is not as happy as the music implied. The move into minor brings about a complete change of character within eight measures: the opening motive for the words "Quanto e felice" is here used for "questo contento," but set in F# minor it does not strike the same joyful note. The music continues to move to the dominant of F# minor and a fermata on the final syllable of "inganno" (deceit) provides a wonderful opportunity for the singer to ornament her line.

Illustration 4.5b: *Quanto è felice*, mm 83-97

The rest of the B section repeats the last two lines of the verse: torment and deceit. Here, all of the instruments torment the voice with their repeated sixteenth notes (Illus. 4.5c). Notable too is the use of the first violin: for much of the aria it is *colla voce* (see 4.5a, m. 22), but from mm 90-102 it leaves this role to provide counterpoint and contrast to the voice.

Illustration 4.5c: *Quanto è felice*, mm 98-109

The lament *Prendi l'ultimo addio* (Illustration 4.6a) shows the young composer's ability to set this type of text as well. A *largo cantabile* tempo helps to establish the mood of a tearful farewell. "Prendi" (take) is set off from the rest of the line by a rest, as if by a sigh. This rest = sigh motif occurs throughout, setting off—in another example—"ch'io moro" (that I die) from "a te fedel" (faithful to you). As one might expect, the sense of longing and desire to linger is expressed on the word "l'ultimo" (the last) through lengthened note values. Even the word "addio" (farewell) has its own motif: a neighbor-note figure.

Illustration 4.6a: *Prendi l'ultimo addio*, mm 6-11

This neighbor note figure (Illus 4.6a, m. 10) will later appear inverted in the bass in both the A section (Illus. 4.6b, mm. 16 and 17) and in the B section (Illus. 4.6d, m. 39). Likewise, the motif on "moro" (I die) in measure 15—a descending leap of a fourth over a descending bass—is developed in the B section, where it becomes a descending leap of a sixth on "morte" (death, Illus. 4.6c, mm. 35 and 36). Further on, a descending stepwise figure in the bass which, to my ear, sounds like melting, illustrates the soul's oppression (m. 39).

Illustration 4.6b: *Prendi l'ultimo addio*, mm 12-17

Illustration 4.6c: *Prendi l'ultimo addio*, mm 32-37

Illustration 4.6d: *Prendi*, mm 38-41

Each of the six arias is composed of two quatrains, which is standard for the *da capo* aria of this period. The rhyme scheme is a b b c, except in *Non parlarmi,* which is a a b c. Maria Antonia uses a variety of verse forms: *quinari* (lines of five syllables), *ottonari* (lines of eight syllables) and *settenari* (lines of seven syllables), the most popular being *settenari.*[54] The quatrains follow the same form of three *versi piani* followed by one *verso tronco.* The *verso tronco* serves to conclude the poetic idea of the quatrain, and musically, serves a strong cadence better than do *versi piani.*

These works share several features with arias from the 1730s and 40s. This was a time when composers were expanding the musical and dramatic possibilities of the *da capo* aria through variations in its form, and in the meter and tempi within it. Typical for Maria Antonia's work at this time is a straightforward text declamation which never allows the music to outshine the text. Attention to poetic and syllabic stress are as important to her as to any good composer or poet. In many ways, however, this set of arias reads like a miniature version of *Il trionfo della fedeltà,* with its loyal shepherds and distressed nymphs. Maria Antonia would return to pastoral themes in her poetry for the court of Dresden, especially those texts set by Ristori.

Early Dresden Texts: Settings by Hasse and Ristori

Upon her arrival in Dresden, Maria Antonia joined the family's chamber music evenings, and further developed her talents as a poet. Her first creative endeavor in Dresden was to write dedicatory cantatas to the King and Queen. These were set by their favorite composer, Johann Adolf Hasse. Hasse had first made the acquaintance of Maximilian III Joseph and Maria Antonia during his July 1746 visit to

---

54 The "classic" Italian verse form is considered the *endecasillabo* (eleven syllables), with the *settenario* being considered the second highest verse form. See *New Grove Opera,* "Versification."

Munich. There, he accompanied them at the harpsichord in chamber performances: Maximilian III Joseph on the bass viol and Maria Antonia singing. Following her marriage to Friedrich Christian, Maria Antonia had Hasse set her texts written for the name days of her parents-in-law. These became the cantatas *Grande Augusto* and *Che ti dirò, Regina?* which Maria Antonia sang herself on 3 August and 8 December, respectively (Illustrations 4.7a-l and 4.8a-g).[55] Hasse is assumed to have been one of Maria Antonia's composition teachers; however, I was unable to verify this supposition.

Illustration 4.7a: *Grande Augusto*, Opening Recitative, mm 1-6

The texts Maria Antonia provided Hasse were in the tradition of occasional poetry, and highly ceremonial in style. Only those with

---

55 Maria Antonia's influence on musical life in Dresden can be seen in the decision to engage Niccolo Porpora as her voice teacher shortly thereafter. He was named Kapellmeister on 13 April 1748 and remained there until 1 January 1752. Perhaps remembering Veracini and the Italian opera "scandal" of 1720, the King appointed Porpora only as Maria Antonia's singing teacher and only for a specific amount of time. Furthermore, he promoted Hasse to the position of *Oberkapellmeister* in 1750. Porpora went on to a post in Vienna, undoubtedly through some help from Maria Antonia.

familial or friendship ties to the court would have known of the existence of these cantatas. They are in manuscript and were never printed, nor were their performances mentioned in newspapers or journals.

In poetic terms, the cantata texts alternate passages in free verse with quatrains of *settenari*. The quatrains have a rhyme scheme of a b b c, and in general share the features of the texts in Maria Antonia's earlier arias. By now, the Princess has developed considerably as a poet, in that she is now able to compose recitatives. The character expressed in each of these texts is Maria Antonia, the dutiful daughter. There is no place for irony here, rather these are dramatic monologues expressing love, respect, and desire. In both, the singer/poet has a lower status than the object of affection: the King is someone to be feared and respected (the fear is that he might withhold his love from his new daughter); the Queen is a mother who receives her new daughter's devotion. Interestingly, the Queen is not addressed by name, but the King is.

In both settings, Hasse has a keen understanding of Maria Antonia's singing style: her love of leaps to f" and g" followed by a descending line, long melismas, high tessitura.[56] One might expect the cantata for the King to have a larger instrumental palette than that for the Queen, but this is not the case. The opening recitative for *Grande Augusto* (Illus. 4.7a, page 1 of the recitative) is *accompagnato* (for strings and voice), and the first aria is likewise scored for string orchestra and voice. The aria is *dal segno*, in common time, and moves along at a stately pace (*Lento*), changing to cut time with the pace quickening (to *Andantino*) for the B section.

---

56 A note about notes: In the tablature I use in this and subsequent chapters, a note name followed by a stroke indicates its placement in the scale. For example, c' is shorthand for middle C (one-line-c); f' is the f a fourth above middle C, and f" is an octave above that, etc.

Illustration 4.7b: *Grande Augusto*, First Aria, mm 9-16

The leaps upward of a fourth and an octave emphasize the words "Te" (Thee) and "adorato" (Illus. 4.7c). The leap up to g" on "adorato" (adored, Illus. 4.7b, mm. 13 and 15) is repeated on "a Te" (Illus. 4.7c, mm. 18 and 22). Long melismatic passages emphasize "palesar" (disclose, Illus. 4.7d, mm. 42-44) and "spiegar" (express, Illus. 4.7e, mm. 83-84).

Illustration 4.7c, *Grande Augusto*, First Aria, mm 17-24

Illustration 4.7d: *Grande Augusto*, "palesar"

Illustration 4.7e: *Grande Augusto*, "spiegar"

Illustration 4.7f: *Grande Augusto*, Second Recitative, mm 1-15

The second recitative begins with voice and continuo alone, which lends an intimacy to it which echoes the urgency of the text (Illus 4.7f).

Illustration 4.7g: *Grande Augusto*, Second Recitative, *accompagnato* section begins

The drama upon which the poet insists towards the end of the recitative—"Deh non negarmi, o SIRE!"—is emphasized with the introduction of an *accompagnato* section (Illus. 4.7g).

Illustration 4.7h: *Grande Augusto*, Second Aria, "calma"

Flutes are added to the orchestra with the second aria. This aria is *da capo,* and like the first, is in common time. With its fourteen-measure melisma on "calma," (Illus 4.7h and 4.7i, mm. 49-61) it is as much an exercise in breath control as it is an expression of the text.

Illustration 4.7i: *Grande Augusto*, Second Aria, "calma" continued

29

Illustration 4.7j: *Grande Augusto*, Second Aria, "calma" continued

30

The harmony and the melisma move through A major and with the final line of text for the quatrain, arrive at D major. The music for the A section being unusually long, the B section occupies a scant 25 measures of music. In 3/8 and *un poco lento*, a different, shorter melismatic passage is used to illustrate the word "vasto" (wide) at the end of the quatrain.

Illustration 4.7k: *Grande Augusto*, Second Aria, "vasto"

Illustration 4.7l: *Grande Augusto*, Second Aria, "vasto" continued

The Queen's cantata is similar in form but has more instrumental coloring, for example, adding muted flutes in the first aria (Illus. 4.8b, "Flauti con sordini"). As in *Grande Augusto*, the opening recitative uses string orchestra and continuo to support the voice.

Illustration 4.8a: *Che ti dirò, Regina?*, Opening Recitative, mm 1-7

Illustration 4.8b: *Che ti dirò, Regina?*, First Aria, mm 1-8, "Flauti...co' sordini"

The first aria is in D major, 6/8 time and *Lento*. The music is lilting and gentle, emphasizing "Cara Genetrice" rather than the "ciel severo" spoken about in the opening line (Illus. 4.8c).

Illustration 4.8c: *Che di dirò, Regina?*, First Aria, mm 9-17, "Cara Genitrice" motif in strings and voice

"Ritrovarla" receives special emphasis through an extended melisma (Illus. 4.8d & e, mm. 23-29 & mm. 28-37).

Illustration 4.8d: *Che ti dirò, Regina?*, First Aria, "ritrovarla"

Illustration 4.8e: *Che ti dirò, Regina?*, First Aria, "ritrovarla" continued

The B section (*allegretto*, in 3/8, Illus. 4.8f), uses the "Cara Genetrice" motif with new text.

Illustration 4.8f: *Che ti dirò, Regina?*, First Aria, mm 48-62, *Allegretto* in 3/8

Hasse accompanies the opening lines of the second recitative with continuo, then sets the last three lines of text are set apart with interjections by the strings (Illus. 4.8g, h, and i).

Illustration 4.8g: *Che ti dirò, Regina?*, Second Recitative, The strings join

Illustration 4.8h; *Che ti dirò, Regina?*, Second Recitative, *accompagnato* continued

4.8i

Illustration 4.8i: *Che ti dirò, Regina?*, Second Recitative, *accompagnato* continued

The major surprise comes in the instrumental forces for the second aria. Not only flutes, but also oboes and horns are added to the texture (Illus. 4.8j).

Illustration 4.8j: *Che ti dirò, Regina?*, Second Aria, mm 1-8

The *allegro* F major aria, in a dancing 3/8 is another *da capo* aria of great length (284 measures). It emphasizes the word "il mio contento" with a melody that undulates gently up and down. The opening ritornello is 27 measures of contentment before the voice joins in the fun (Illus. 4.8k).

Illustration 4.8k, *Che ti dirò, Regina?*, Second Aria, mm 28-36

Hasse would only set one other poetic work of Maria Antonia's, *La conversione di Sant'Agostino*. When Maria Antonia began to write pastoral poetry and poetry based on classical myths, she no longer chose Hasse as her collaborator, for reasons that no sources clarify. Perhaps this was due to his constant absences from court, making him unavailable. But more likely is that Maria Antonia had begun to study composition with someone who may have reminded her of her teacher in Munich: Giovanni Ristori.

At the time of Maria Antonia's entry into Dresden, Giovanni Alberto Ristori had long been the chamber organist at court, and in 1746 had been appointed to the title of Church Composer. Much of

Ristori's music was lost to war—the bombardments by Prussia in 1760 as well as World War II. There are eight extant cantatas by Ristori, three of which are settings of texts by Maria Antonia and date from 1748 and 1749. In all three of her cantata texts, the active voice is that of a woman: It is Nice who laments and creates the drama in *Nice e Tirsi*; it is Lavinia who speaks to Turno in *Lavinia a Turno*; it is Dido who expresses her outrage in *Didone Abbandonata.* I will examine his setting of one of these, her *Nice e Tirsi* (Illustration 4.9).

Illustration 4.9a: *Nice e Tirsi*, First Recitative, mm 1-6, "Ah! Crudo Amore!"

Another reason for my choice of this cantata for analysis is that the characters of Nice and Tirsi will later appear in Maria Antonia's first opera, *Il trionfo della fedeltà*. With this text and her others on pastoral and classical themes, Maria Antonia develops the ideas previously expressed in her six arias: love and fidelity. Now she places herself squarely in the company of authors such as Guarini. In her cantata texts as in her entire poetic output, Maria Antonia positions women front and center. They are active characters, and do not wait to be rescued. They remain defiant; they seek to receive love and respect on their terms. They are neither comic nor satirical.

Ristori was an ideal choice to set Maria Antonia's pastoral texts, as a composer of such operas as *Pallade trionfante in Arcadia* (1713) and others based on classical mythology or pastoral themes. *Nice e Tirsi* is subtitled: *Cantata a voce sola co'strum:^{ti} / e un oboe conc:^{to} / di Ermelinda Talea. / posta in Musica da Gio: Alberto Ristori*. / Dresda 1749.

The first aria contains quatrains composed of *ottonari*.[57] The first recitative (*accompagnato*) has the tempo marking *poco andante e affetuoso*, and the gentle sixteenth-note descending-ascending figuration sets a peaceful mood in the opening nine measures (Illus. 4.9a). When the voice exclaims, "Ah! Cruel Love! What have I ever done to you?", the strings fall silent momentarily (Illus 4.9a, m. 3), and then interject short passages at various points in the text to punctuate a word or phrase (Illus. 4.9b: m. 8 after "perche tanto rigor contro al cor mio?", for instance).

Illustration 4.9b: *Nice e Tirsi*, First Recitative, mm 7-12

The first aria is in C minor, and common time. Again, the desired feeling is *affetuoso*. Grief ("duolo") can be heard in the repetition of the first few words as well as in its key (Illus. 4.9c).

Illustration 4.9c: *Nice e Tirsi*, First Aria, mm 1-7; "Non v'è duolo"

Ristori responds to the text in another way which brings out both the beauty of the poetry and its meaning: the last two lines of the first stanza are set off from the first two by a change in meter from duple to triple (Illus. 4.9d).

Illustration 4.9d: *Nice e Tirsi*, First Aria, duple to triple meter

This happens again in the second stanza, where the text is set even more syllabically than in the first stanza. A momentary move to A-flat major for "l'infelice" (the unhappiness) highlights that word. The last line of the stanza is repeated for emphasis and, as in Maria Antonia's early arias, the strings, continuo and voice end on a unison. For the second recitative, the voice and continuo are alone for the first six lines of text (mm. 1-9). Then the strings join in to emphasize "abborrisca" and "detesti" (abhorrent, detested) with descending runs and a change to *a tempo giusto e staccato*. When Nice again views her beloved, the music softens. Ascending tutti strings harmonize for "ma che veggio" (but what do I see) and "qual gioia" (what joy) and the tempo moderates upon "Tirsi ritorna a me fedel" (Tirsi returns faithful to me). The next lines are mostly for voice and continuo, with the tempo slowing to *lento* for the last five lines, as Nice begs Amor's forgiveness. The oboe doubles the first violin for the final aria (in G major, and common time), and there is quite a bit of motifs exchange between the oboe/first violin and the second violin. The upward leap of a sixth for "E' d'amor" (Illus. 4.9e) is the same upward leap as in the first aria for "non v'è duolo".

Illustration 4.9 e: "È d'amor" leap

Again the emphasis on certain words does not overpower the structure of the poetic text; "fa scordare," "tormento," and "penar" invite a treatment in music, offering the opportunity for wonderful dissonances and fast note values.

Maria Antonia continued to write poetry, mostly in French, and continued her studies of dramatic composition. Circa 1750 she translated Metastasio's version of *Demetrio* into French and performed it, along with other members of the court, perhaps set to her own music.[58] A collection of French language poetry entitled *Poesies D'E: T:* (for Ermelinda Talea) shows her continuing to mix poetry and music. Due to its use of her Arcadian name, the collection obviously dates from after 1747. It contains a cantata dedicated to the Queen, "Le Siege de Troie" for a solo voice, put into music by the Princess, in the Italian style.[59] Unfortunately, the music does not survive.

French poetry set to music in the Italian style was a practice Maria Antonia apparently learned during her studies with Ferrandini, whose own "Opera Francese" was one of Maria Antonia's favorite works.[60] Other poetry in this collection which draws upon classical themes is *Daphne à Tircis*, another pastoral. Ever eager to experiment with form, she wrote this pastoral in the form of a minuet and trio.[61] Other poems in this collection include one written for her son, Friedrich August, an impromptu for her spouse Friedrich Christian,[62] and others on the themes of love. The Roman gods who find their stories retold through Maria Antonia's eyes include *Venus et Adonis* and *Jupiter et Semele*. Increasingly, however, Maria Antonia worked on her most ambitious

---

58 Libretto in D: Dlb, Handschriftenabteilung.

59 Le Siege de Troïe / Cantade / à une voix seule/mise en musique dans le gout italien.

60 Judging by its inclusion in her catalog and her having brought it to Dresden.

61 *Daphne à Tircis* is a *Menuet/qui se chante alternativement avec le trio ci joint à coté* (Minuet/to be sung alternatively with the adjoining trio).

62 One of the activities upon which members of the Arcadian Academy prided themselves was the ability to extemporize poetry and music.

project: a pastoral opera dedicated to the King. This is the subject of my next chapter.

Grande Augusto

Recit: Grande Augusto,

ricevi frà tanti ardenti voti,

che in tal Giorno per Te s'alzano al cielo

d'una tua Figlia ancor gli umili accenti.

Scusa l'ardir, che il core sprona il labbro

a cantar i Tuoi gran preggi.

Ma che fò? Come mai potrò

de' Merti Tuoi degna lode trovar!

Io, che non sono capace a verseggiar,

che del Parnasso non ebbi mai l'ingresso?

Ahi! Che questo pensier muta mi rende

vengo de detti miei a chiederti pietà.

Scusa tai versi, sol rimira il core

pien d'ossequio per Te, e pien d'amore.

Aria: Io non sò trovare accenti,

adorato Genitore,

onde io possa a Te del core

tutti i voti palesar.

Deh Tu stesso in que' momenti

leggi e spiega nel mio petto

questo tenero rispetto,

che il mio cor non sà spiegar.

Recit: Sì, leggi nel mio core i voti,

che per Te sparge quest'alma

che la mia debolezza sforza il labbro a tacer.

Ma Tu che sai con qual rispetto io t'amo,

facilmente potrai il mio silenzio interpretar.

Timore è quel, che mi trattien;

Ma pur Ti chiedo in questo Giorno un dono,

che in un Dì sì felice sò, che nulla si niega.

Dunque spero ottener quel, che domando.

La mia felicità sì ne dipende,

che non puoi ricusar al cor divoto quel,

ch'è dell'alma mia unico voto.

Deh non negarmi, o SIRE!

il Tuo Paterno amore: questo è il Dono,

che a Te chiede de il mio core.

Aria: Sì, questo è il solo dono,

che fà contenta l'alma

questo di dolce calma

sol riempisce il sen.

Se mi dai questo io sono

l'alma più fortunata,

che mai possa esser nata

in sul vasto terren.

Translation of *Grande Augusto*

Recit: Great Augustus,

        receive among so many ardent vows,

        that on such a Day for Thee are raised to heaven

        from one of thy Daughters still the humble accents.

        Pardon the boldness, that the heart spurs the lip

        to sing Thy great praises.

        But what shall I do? How will I ever be able

        of Thy merits worthy praise to find!

        I, who am incapable of ever making verses,

        who of Parnassus never had admittance?

        Ah! That this thought renders me mute

        I come to ask thy mercy for what I am about to say.

        Pardon such verses, but only focus upon the heart

        full of reverence for Thee, and full of love.

Aria: I know not how to find the words

        beloved Parent,

        through which I can disclose to Thee

        all the offerings of my heart

        Prithee Thyself in those moments

        read and see outlined in my breast

        this tender respect

        that my heart knows not how to explain.

Recit: Yes, read in my heart the offerings,

        that for Thee this soul scatters

        that my weakness forces the lip to be silent.

But Thou who knowest with what respect I love Thee,

canst easily interpret my silence.

Fear is that, which restrains me;

But yet I ask of Thee on this Day a gift,

because on a Day so happy I know that nothing is denied.

Therefore I hope to obtain that which I ask for.

My happiness so depends on it,

That thou canst not refuse to a devoted heart that

which is, from the soul, my only desire.

Oh, deny me not, oh SIRE!

Thy Fatherly love: this is the Gift,

that from Thee I ask from my heart.

Aria: Yes, this is the only gift

that makes happy the soul

this sweet calm

alone replenishes the breast.

If you give me this I am

the luckiest soul

That ever could have been born

in this wide world.

Che ti dirò, Regina?

Recit: Che ti dirò, Regina?

        Non ti voglio stancar colli miei voti.

        Già tanti ne ricevi,

        che in questo Dì inutile saria il dir,

        quel che per Te sente il mio core.

        Già si, con qual rispetto

        quel core a Te sarà sempre divoto.

        Altro, più non dirò.

        Solo m'accingo la sorte a ringraziar,

        che il ciel cortese tutto quel,

        che mi tolse in Te mi rese.

Aria: Mi tolse il ciel severo

        la cara Genitrice,

        Ma quanto son felice

        nel ritrovarla in Te.

        In Te trovar già spero

        di Madre il dolce amore,

        che d'umil Figlia il core

        tu sempre avrai da me.

Recit: Sì, che da Te ricevo di bontade,

        e d'amor prove sì grandi;

        che non potrei bramar più del tuo core;

        ma come meritar cotanto amore?

        Sò, cara Genetrice,

che di tanta bontà degna non sono;

deggio solo al Tuo cor un sì gran dono.

Ma, se rendermi degna già non potrei

d'un così gran favore almen sempre sarà

grato il mio core.

Aria: Il Tuo amor è il mio contento,

per Te sono ognor felice,

se da Te sperarmi lice

questo eccesso di bontà.

Che nel cor per Te risento,

tanto amor, tanto rispetto,

che già mai in altro petto

moto ugual si troverà.

Translation of *Che ti dirò, Regina?*

Recit: What will I say to you, Queen?

        I do not wish to tire you with my avowals.

        Already so many you receive,

        that on this Day useless it would be to say,

        what for Thee my heart feels.

        Already yes, with what respect

        that heart to Thee will always be devoted.

        Moreover, more I will not say.

        I only prepare myself to thank fate,

        that everything that the gracious heaven

        took from me, in Thee, it restores to me.

Aria: Taken from me the stern heavens

        the dear Parent,

        but how happy I am

        in finding her again in Thee.

        In Thee I already hope to find

        of a Mother the sweet love,

        that from a humble Daughter's heart

        thou wilt always have from me.

Recit: Yea, that from Thee I receive of goodness,

        and of love proofs so great;

        that I could not crave more from thy heart;

        but how to deserve such love?

        I know, dear Parent,

that of so much goodness I am not worthy;

I only deign to Thy heart so great a gift.

But, if I already could not make myself worthy

of so great a favor, at least always shall be

forever grateful my heart.

Aria: Thy love is my contentment

For Thee I am every day happy,

If from Thee I may hope

this excess of goodness.

That in my heart for Thee I feel,

so much love, so much respect,

that never in another breast

will one find equal emotion.

Nice e Tirsi

Recit: Ah! Crudo Amore! Io che ti feci mai?

Perchè tanto rigor contro al cor mio?

Tu mi feristi appena,

che nella piaga incrudelir ti sento.

Aggiungi pena a pena,

e par che goda ancor del mio tormento

Dall'istante che Tirsi

s'offerse ai sguardi miei

al tuo Impero mi resi

Egli giurò d'amarmi,

Io la fiam[m]a del cor non gli celai.

E tu, ch'esser dovresti

propizio a tanto amor,

crudel, tu stesso t'ascondi a gli occhi miei,

Lungi dal mio Tesoro passo

afflitta i miei dì

ne posso almeno saper se pensa a me,

chi m'arde il seno.

Aria: Non v'è duolo uguale al mio

amo Tirsi e non poss'io

più vederlo e dirgli almeno

t'amo fida, e avere in seno

non sospiro che il tuo cor

Forse oh Dio! Che ad altra amante

giura infido amor costante?

forse già della sua Nice

si scordò... Nò. L'infelice

m'ama e pena al mio dolor

Recit: Ma già che il crudo Amore

non può dar che tormento,

se non posso sperar le sue catene almen,

farò palese il suo rigore

perche l'odio divenga d'ogni core.

Senza incensi il suo Alzar sempre rimanga

ogn'alma l'abborrisca,

ogn'uno lo detesti

e perquel Dio crudel più non si pianga.

Ninfe, Pastori udite

d'amor non vi fidate.

Il disleale promette lusinghiero

e gioia e pace al cor; ma non è vero

crederlo a me potete;

Io che misera sono

per servire all'alteir,

con quest'inganno mi rapì l'amante;

forse ad altri il donò, lo fè incostante.

Di tutte le mie pene

esso è l'unico Autor...

Ma che vegg'io! Qual gioia!

Qual piacere, ecco il mio Bene!

Il mio caro Tirsi ritorna a me fedel.

Pietoso Amore! Tu lo rendi al mio cor

quanto mi pento dell'ingiuste querele

che per troppo dolor sciolse il mio labbro.

Perdona ad un'amante i delirÿ del cor

sotto il tuo giogo sempre viver vogl'io

e quanto più di te l'alma insensata

sino ad or si lagnò,

tanto più grata il tuo vantar

saprà soave Impero

sin che ti sia soggetto il Mondo intero.

Aria: E d'amor dolce l'Impero

che sebben sembra severo

fa scordare in un momento

il tormento ed il penar.

Se più spene non sovrasta

del suo Bene un guardo basta

onde fugga ogni timore

ne si pensa che ad amar.

Translation of *Nice e Trisi*

Recit: Ah! Cruel Love! What did I ever do to thee?

Why so much rigor against my heart?

No sooner didst Thou wound me,

than in the wound I feel thy wrath.

Heaping pain upon pain,

and you seem to rejoice from my torment.

From the instant that Tirsi

offered himself to my gaze

I entered your realm.

He swore that he loved me,

I did not conceal from him the flame in my heart.

And Thou, who shouldst be

propitious to so much love,

cruel one, thou thyself hidest thyself from my eyes,

Far from my Treasure I pass

my days afflicted

unable in the least to know if he thinks of me,

he who inflames my breast.

Aria: There is no sorrow equal to mine

I love Tirsi and I cannot

see him anymore, and tell him at least

I love thee faithfully and have in my breast

no other sigh than your heart.

Perhaps, oh God! That to another lover

he unfaithfully swears constant love

Perhaps already about his Nice

has forgotten... No. The unhappy one

Loves me and pities my sorrow.

Recit: But since cruel Love

cannot give that torment,

if I cannot hope to be released from its chains,

I will make clear his rigors

so that hatred will grow in every heart.

Without incense let his Alzar always remain

let every soul abhor him,

let everyone detest him

and for that cruel God let no more weep.

Nymphs, Shepherds hear

of love, trust ye not.

The disloyal one promises flattering

and joy and peace to the heart; but it is not true

believe it from me you can;

I who am miserable

from serving the disdainful one,

with this liar my beloved robbed me;

perhaps to another he gave it, his faith inconstant.

Of all my pains

it is the only Author...

But what do I see? What joy!

What pleasure! Here is my darling!

My dear Tirsi returns to me faithful.

Merciful Love! Thou renderest him to my heart

how much I repent of my unjust querulousness

that from an overdose of sorrow escaped my lips.

Pardon a lover the deliriums of the heart

under thy yoke always I want to live,

And how much more of thee the senseless soul

till now has lamented,

the more grateful thy boasting

will know sweet empire

as long as the whole World is subject to thee.

Aria: It is of sweet love the Empire

which although it seems severe

makes one forget in a moment

The torment and the pain.

If the pains are not overpowered

from his Goodness one look is enough,

so that every fear flees

when one thinks of loving.

Chapter 5
Opera Seria, Intermezzo, or Pastoral?

By the mid-18th century, the prevailing popular style of opera was *opera seria,* which from Vienna to Venice and beyond became identified with libretti written by Pietro Metastasio. Plots featuring heroic characters drawn from classical mythology, a benevolent ruler, and a happy ending usually through the actions of said ruler were de rigueur.

Other genres such as the pastoral and the intermezzo were considered lighter entertainment forms. Intermezzi were often performed between the acts of a *seria* performance (hence the English term "intermission"). The intermezzo drew its characters from the commedia dell'arte, a genre which, though it made the monarchs laugh, was often considered suspect, given its penchant for biting social and political satire. The pastoral offered the nobility an escape from the cares of city life and could fit musically and dramatically between the other two operatic genres.

Unlike the *seria*-style work, the tragedies that occur in the pastoral are not those of nations under threat of war or of kingdoms ruthlessly stolen by the brother of the heir to the throne. The tragedies are on a simple human scale: love sought, love betrayed, love attained. The quintessential pastorals from the Renaissance that were to inform the genre during the Baroque period are Torquato Tasso's *Aminta* (1581) and G. B. Guarini's *Il pastor fido* (1589). These were both essentially court dramas, and inspired madrigals based on their subject matter. They were performed by the lords and ladies of the court, with minimal scenery, and were strictly for the amusement of the nobles, not the public. Guarini's *Il pastor fido* remained the model for pastorals in the 17th century, and was translated into most European languages, the first German version appearing in 1671.[63] On into the 18th century, characters with names like Clori, Silvio, Dorilla, Fileno and Tirsi appear in poetry and in serenatas, cantatas, and pastoral operas.

Unlike the intermezzo, the pastoral's characters are not parodies of doctors, lawyers, merchants, or nobles. They may be simple shepherds and shepherdesses, yet they possess the highest courtly values. They are graceful, elegant, and noble, not the comic characters typical of commedia dell'arte. Nor were they satirical. They also tended to be nondescript: any number of Tirsis, Nices, Filenos have graced the pages of these dramas. It is set entirely in Arcadia, that paradise where all are free from the woes of city and court life, and where love is independent of duty. Here in Arcadia, love is shielded from the demands of society. This sort of freedom was often denied to women in early modern European society.

In a highly regulated world where dynastic considerations took precedence over emotional ties, marriages were matters of economic and political alliance. It should come as no surprise that pastoral poetry was, at some level, considered the rightful property of women in the

---

63 For more on the pastoral in Germany, see Harris, *Handel and the Pastoral Tradition.*

nobility. This genre, more than *opera seria*, may have given female nobility a socially acceptable outlet for their creativity.[64]

Evidence of Maria Antonia's interest in theater and in pastoral literature is clearly documented in her library. The library can be glimpsed as it stood at the end of her lifetime through a catalog made after her death. The books Maria Antonia brought with her from Munich and accumulated in Dresden show more than any other source the range of her knowledge and her interests. The layout and organization of the catalog encourage its being read as reflecting the ordering of Maria Antonia's library. Most of its contents became part of what is now the Sächsische Landes- und Universitätsbibliothek (SLUB),[65] and some of it is now part of the Hauptstaatsarchiv. An overview of its thousands of volumes shows us the kinds of knowledge a highly educated female noble would be expected to have in the middle 18th century. It is probable that this catalog does not even list every document ever perused by the Electress.

As can be seen from the table below, the largest section of Maria Antonia's library consisted of texts in History (104 pages), followed by Literature (38 pages), Science (36 pages), Theology (34 pages), Novels (25 pages), Theater (19 pages) and Philosophy (18 pages). Most of the titles are French and reflect upon her education, which included a thorough grounding in French history, language, and literature. This was standard procedure for the children of the nobility, as France was the dominant military and cultural power in Europe from the late 17th century. This dominance only began to be challenged later in the 18th century. Just as the linguistic preference of the nobility was French, so does French history and literature dominate the catalog. The section dealing with histories of France is 19 pages in length, the longest section

---

64   Although I know of no such study, it seems a topic ripe for scholarship. Sophie Charlotte of Prussia (d. 1705) wrote pastoral poetry, and I am certain that a search in other archives would yield a wealth of material on this subject.

65   See D: Dla, Loc. 30541. Stipulation die Einrichtung der Secundo-Genitur betr. 1776.

devoted to a single country. In Literature, French authors stake their claim on 13 pages compared to an average of nine pages for literature from other countries. There are 13 pages of French plays compared to three each for Italian and German, and most of the Novels are French. Her knowledge of several languages besides French is visible in the catalog, which includes numerous titles in Italian, German, Latin, English and Spanish.[66]

Maria Antonia's Library

In the original catalog, sections are divided by book format, from largest to smallest: Folio, Quarto, Octavo and Duodecimo. Listings for individual works are given in this order: Title, Number of Parts, Author, Publisher, Place of publication, Date, Number of volumes. If manuscript, then "Ms" takes the place of any other information.

I.
Theologie (p. 2)
Histoire (p. 37)
Histoire Universelle, Genealogie, Chronologie (p. 37)
Histoire ancienne et Antiquités (p. 51)
Histoire generale d'Allemagne, et de la Maison d'Autriche (p. 64)
Histoire de Baviére (p. 70)
Histoire de Saxe (p. 78)
Maisons d'Allemagne (p. 81)
Histoire de France (p. 82)
Histoire d'Espagne, de Portugal, d'Italie (p. 101)
Histoire d'Angleterre, d'Hollande, et des Païs du Nord (p. 110)
Histoire de la Turquie et des Païs hors de l'Europe (p. 129)
Oeuvres historiques mêlées (p. 133)
Geographie (p. 141)

66　Maria Antonia also spoke English, as attested to by Burney.

The first book listed in the catalog is the Bible, which, presumably had pride

of place in Maria Antonia's physical library as well. It is in two editions: the *Biblia sacra, vulgatae editionis Sixti V.* published in Venice in 1720 and *La Sainte Bible en Latin et en françois, avec notes litterales* by Mr. De Sacy (in four parts) published in Paris in 1717. These may have been among Maria Antonia's earliest reading material, given their dates.

The rest of the theology section is a mixture of books on individual saints' lives and on the laws of the church. There are fifteen books on St. Augustine, more than on other saints, including her patron saint, St. Anthony, or on the Virgin Mary. Approximately half of the books in this section are in Italian, with the rest divided among French, Latin, and German (eight pages of books are in German script). Included in her library were her own translations of the Miserere (*Sentimens d'une Ame*), and *Theatrum affectum humanorum* by the Jesuit priest Fritz Lang, a teacher of eloquence and acting in Munich.[67]

Her collection of works by classical authors included Virgil, whose *Aneid* appears in several editions, Ovid's *Metamorphosis*, writings by Heroditus, Cicero, Homer, Tacitus, Aristotle, and Sappho. Quintilian's book on oration also found a place in her library.

Among the French works found in the Belles Lettres section are books by Racine, Rousseau, Voltaire, as well as the French translations of Erasmus' *In Praise of Folly*. Italian authors included in Belles Lettres are Petrarch, Dante, Tasso, and Guarini in addition to Metastasio and Apostolo Zeno.

Her libretto to *Talestri* is included here in multiple copies, as is the 1772 publication of her collected libretti *Vari componimenti della musica di E.T.P.A.* Oddly, no copies of *Il trionfo della fedeltà* appear to

---

67 See *The Art of Gesture* for more on this aspect of 18th century drama.

have been in her library.[68] Guarini's *Il pastor fido* and Tasso's *Aminta* are among the works in her Italian literature collection. Multiple copies of each of these two Renaissance pastoral dramas suggest a special interest in these works. Also appearing in this section are works by various members of the Arcadian Academy.

Her "Ouevres Melees" contains such varied works as two books of predictions by Nostradamus, a book of games, a book on divination, and books of humorous anecdotes. Also are editions of *Le Mercure Hollandois* (1672-1676), a journal much like *Le Mercure de France*, a publication of the most interesting cultural events occurring at the courts and in the palaces of the nobility. *Les Femmes illustres, ou les Harangues heroiques* by Mr. De Scudery (Lyon, 1660) likewise found its way onto these shelves.

The theater section is opened by a manuscript copy, in French, of Metastasio's *Demetrio*; it is among the works wrongly attributed to Maria Antonia. Other authors found here are Diderot, Voltaire, Corneille, Marivaux, Favart, Racine, as well as those known in music circles as Jean-Baptiste Lully's librettists, Molière and Quinault. Her wide-ranging theatrical interests included street theater: an early collection of works performed in Paris in the open air *Nouveau Theatre de la Foire* (Pairs, 1758, in four volumes) is part of her collection. *Detail d'un divertissement* (Dresden, 1763), in which Maria Antonia was installed as the Tenth Muse during Carnival 1763, is among the works here. Italian and English theatrical works in their French translations are part of her library, as well as two volumes on the Bavarian theater *Theatre Bavarois* (Augsburg, 1755). Numerous French opera libretti were also collected by the Electress.

---

68 A music catalog of her son Friedrich August's library has a section listing books he inherited from Maria Antonia. Among these are several copies of the Breitkopf scores to *Trionfo* and *Talestri*.

A book of interest to theater historians today for the clues it gives to performance practice was of interest to Maria Antonia: *Teatro Italiano* by Martello (1715). Also in the Italian theater section are the dramatic poems of Zeno and Metastasio, comedies by Pietro Chiari, Carlo Goldoni, and dramatic works by Pietro Bernardoni.

A small section of German theater works rounds out the Theater section. Six out of its 41 books date from 1749 or earlier, six date from 1754-55, and the rest date from 1759 or later, most being from the 1770s. Gottsched's *Deutsche Schaubühne* (Leipzig, 1746) is here.

Maria Antonia shared the literary interests of her age when it came to her wide-ranging collection of novels. Larger works of fiction such as versions of *Don Quixote* in Spanish, Italian, and French open this section. These are followed by novels about nobility of the past, then novels consisting of fictional letters (*Lettres de...*). Then there are French translations of English-language historical novels involving English nobility. A few historical novels published in France in the late 17th century are also here, as is a collection of fictional memoirs. A section of German novels rounds out the collection, the earliest of which dates from 1764.

Sprinkled throughout Maria Antonia's library are works by women. They vary from works of poetry such as *Poesies de Made et Madlle Deshoulières*, a published collection of letters from the Marquise de Sevigné, fiction such as *La Muse Limonadiére* by Madame Bourette, and a *Receuil de Pieces galantes* by the Comtesse de la Suze (1695). The theater section contains *Theatre à l'usage des jeunes Gens* by a Madame Genlis (Paris, 1749 in four volumes), *Theatre de Mademoiselle Barbier* (Paris, 1745) as well as a translation of contemporary theatrical works by Elisab:[etta] Caminer (Venice, 1772). There is even a work by a fellow female Arcadian: *Rime di Oriana Ecalidea P. A.* Published in Berlin, 1760.[69]

The breadth and depth of this library shows Maria Antonia to have had an interest in literature and the arts surpassing that of most women of her station. This is perhaps not surprising when one realizes that her Catholicism grew out of a Jesuit-influenced environment. This order stressed education and promoted the edifying powers of the arts and encouraged their active cultivation. Through her readings, Maria Antonia acquired the knowledge that would enable her to write poetry and later music at a professional level. Her interest in the works of Lang and Martello suggest some training in oration and interest in acting.

She turned her pen to classical mythology and literature and, for her first opera, chose a genre considered appropriate for women: the pastoral. A pastoral's action centers on courtship. It is about the lover—usually defined as male—seeking, winning, losing, and often winning again his (female) beloved. The male is active; the female, by convention, is more sought than seeking. Like most literary genres, the majority of its published interpreters were male. However, female nobility from Sophie Charlotte of Prussia to Wilhelmina of Bayreuth and Maria Antonia turned to this genre for an expression of their creative energies.

No one has yet examined why this genre, rather than the stories of Roman heroes, gods, and goddesses. I posit that there were practical as well as expressive reasons. Pastoral operas and cantatas lend themselves to chamber performance. They require small dramatic forces: in the case of a cantata, one solo voice plus a continuo group or small string ensemble; in the case of an opera, you will have at most two couples. Themes such as love, devotion, self-sacrifice, and honor were considered

---

69 The real name of the author is Veronica Cantelli Tagliazucchi, who was inducted into the Academy by 1744. She is listed on p. 201, *Gli arcadi dal 1690 al 1800: Onomasticon.*

to belong to women. These reasons would explain the attractiveness of this genre for women like Maria Antonia.[70]

When a woman writes a pastoral, it is interesting to see how her perspective fashions the drama. *Il trionfo della fedeltà* differs from the conventions of the genre in that it is women who control the action. The tension of the story comes not from the chase of the nymph by the shepherd but from the betrayal of (women's) friendship and the test of the beloved's fidelity (as the title implies). Furthermore, though the characters of most pastorals may be "elegant nobodies," to quote Ellen Harris, the characters of this dramas are somebodies: the main character, that of Nice, was played—in the work's premiere and in subsequent performances in family circles—by *Trionfo's* librettist and composer, Maria Antonia. As she says herself in the quote that opens the next chapter, the characters were "close to the truth." These are thinly disguised idealizations of Maria Antonia and Friedrich Christian.[71]

This opera can be, and perhaps should be seen as an idealization of the devoted relationship between Maria Antonia and Friedrich Christian. Throughout, Maria Antonia depicts a world in which the sexes are equal in rank and in power. Furthermore, she uses the pastoral as a genre in which Christian mercy and forgiveness can be expressed: the character of Nice forgives Tirsi his supposed trespasses. Tirsi is willing to die to prove his love, although he does not know what offense he committed.

---

70 Even in those courts where the nobles did not write their own entertainments, such as the imperial court of Vienna, the pastoral genre came to be preferred over the large-scale *opera seria* precisely for its use of much smaller forces.

71 Although one needs to beware the danger of identifying the author with her characters—see Kord, *Little Detours*, p. 9ff—Maria Antonia herself seems to have sought this identification. She not only wrote the text and composed the music, but she also sang the role of Nice in chamber performances. It is only later, when she became Electress, that she distanced herself from the character by allowing others to interpret the role.

Sources Consulted

There are two versions of *Il trionfo della fedeltà* that I examined for this study. MT.4.114 is written in a heavy dark ink.[72] The title page reads "Il Trionfo Della Fedeltà: Favola Pastorale," but nowhere on this page does a composer's or librettist's name appear. Its stated performance location is given as "Da rappresentarsi nel Reale Teatro di" with no city, court, or country listed in the inch-and-a-half of blank space remaining between this and the next line which informs us that the performance of this work is "In occasione del felicissimo giorno Natalizio Di S. M. Il Re di Pollonia, &c."

A stamp marks this as being property of the King's Private Music Collection (KPMS or Königliche Privat Musiksammlung), with later stamps informing us that the libretto was also part of the Royal Public Library (KÖB or Königliche Öffentliche Bibliothek) before both collections became part of the Sächsische Landesbibliothek.

From the paper, the handwriting, and binding I have dated this to 1748, and I will refer to it as *Trionfo 1748*. Another manuscript libretto, which differs significantly from *Trionfo 1748*, is the version I will call *Trionfo 1754*.[73] It is written in a lighter ink, and with a more elegant hand (see Illustrations 5.1 and 5.2).

---

72 This is also available under the call number MT.4.115. These two manuscripts do not differ significantly, and so will be considered one and the same for the purposes of this discussion.

73 MT.4.113 Rara

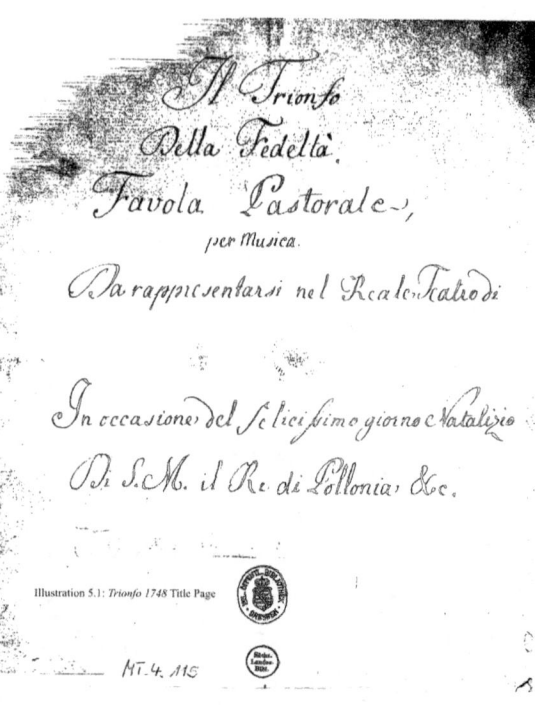

Illustration 5.1: *Trionfo* 1748 Title Page

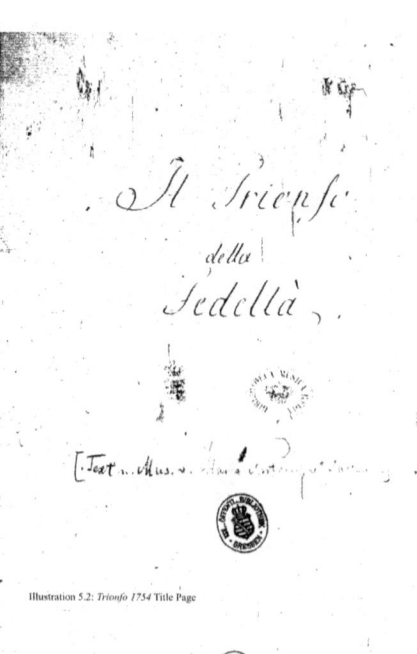

Illustration 5.2: *Trionfo* 1754 Title Page

Again, nowhere does the name of the composer/librettist appear, nor is a performance location or date stated. However, since this libretto does not differ greatly from the printed version or from the text as it appears in the Breitkopf score, I have assigned a date of 1754.

The libretti are both manuscript copies, not in Maria Antonia's hand. The scribe for *T1748* used darker ink, and a heavier hand. That the word "scena" replaces "scene" from the end of Act I to the end of the libretto may indicate that this scribe was Italian. The libretto I call *T1754* is written in a light brown ink, with a much more elegant hand; a hand similar to, but not matching, that of the third part of Maria Antonia's catalog. None of Maria Antonia's biographers have compared these manuscripts, but they reveal exciting insights into her creative process and growth as a poet/composer.

Chapter 6
Her First Opera: *Il trionfo della fedeltà*

L'argomento di questa favola è tutto d'invenzione dell' AUTRICE, benchè
i caratteri fossero allora presi dal vero.

(The plot of this fable is completely the invention of the AUTHOR,
although the characters were close to the truth.)[74]

The Poetic and Dramatic Structure of *Trionfo*

Both c1748 and c1754 are roughly the same in terms of structure.
Both are in three acts. Both versions observe Aristotelian unities of
time and place and take place in the fabled realm of Arcadia within the
span of a day.[75] The characters are the same, and the plot is identical
in its outline: the shepherdess Clori has rejected the affections of the
shepherd Tirsi for those of his rival—later his friend—Fileno. But upon
seeing that the newest shepherdess to arrive in Arcadia, Nice, has won

---

74 *Varj componimenti della musica di E. T. P. A.*, p. 72. The above statement prefaces the
libretto of *Il trionfo della fedeltà* in this 1772 publication.
75 Both Aristotle's *Poetics* and Corneille's version of the same were part of Maria Antonia's
library. As a student of dramatic poetry, she made certain that her operas adhered to these
classical guidelines.

Tirsi's heart, Clori is filled with jealousy. She resolves to break apart this union and win Tirsi back for herself. In the end, Clori's plot is foiled, and Nice and Tirsi remain faithful to each other and very much in love.

Trionfo 1748 contains a page-long "Argomento," which summarizes the plot. The "Interlocutori" are then listed in the following order: Clori, Tirsi, Nice, Fileno. *Trionfo 1754* has no "Argomento" and lists the "Personaggi" in the order Nice, Tirsi, Clori, and Fileno. These changes already presume different attitudes toward an audience: by removing the plot synopsis, one allows the audience to discover the action of the drama while it unfolds. In changing the list of characters, the heroine of the drama assumes a place of importance on the page that she will have on the stage. Another difference is in the descriptions of scenery: the ones in *Trionfo 1748* are more detailed, perhaps pointing to a performance that was performed more as a concert work, that is, semi-staged, rather than as a fully staged and costumed opera.

There are noticeable differences in dramatic conception and in use of language between these two versions of *Trionfo* which support the idea of influence by Arcadian ideals. The table below shows the scene summary of each act for each version.

Comparison of 1748 and 1754 Versions of *Il trionfo della fedeltà*	
c1748	c1754
Atto Pmo [Primo]	**Atto I**
Scena I: Clori e Fileno Aria Fileno: Come un sogno menzognero	Scena 1: Clori e Nice Aria Clori: Si sperar tu sola puoi
Scena II: Clori e Nice Aria Clori: Non temer. Fedel se vuoi	Scena 2: Nice e Tirsi Aria Tirsi: Che vuoi ch'io pensi?
Scena III: Nice e Tirsi Aria Nice: Offri a più vaghi rai	Scena 3: Nice sola Aria: Ah! Per mia pace oh Dio!
Scena IV: Tirsi solo Aria: Ah! Se il mio Bene è solo	
Change of scenery	Change of scenery
Scena V: Fileno e poi Tirsi	Scena 4: Tirsi, e Fileno fra diversi parti
Scena VI: Clori e detti	Scena 5: Clori in disparte, e detti Aria Tirsi: Dille: che fido io sono
Scena VII: Clori e Fileno Aria ileno: Come si lagna se l'augelletto	Scena 6: Fileno e Clori Aria Fileno: Come il miser augelletto
Scena VIII: Clori sola	Scena 7: Clori, e poi Nice Aria Nice: Amato pur se vuoi
Scena IX: Clori e Nice Aria Clori: Tra fiori, e tra le fronde	Scena 8: Clori sola Aria: Veder parmi già il mio
Scena X: Nice sola Aria: Esci mio cor di pena	Fine dell'Atto Primo
Fine dell'Atto Primo	

c1748	c1754
Atto Secondo	**Atto Secondo**
Scena I: Nice e Fileno	Scena 1: Nice, Fileno e poi Tirsi
Scena II: Tirsi e Detti	Scena 2: Tirsi e Nice Aria Nice: Serba per me fedele
Scena III: Tirsi e Nice Aria Nice: Ah rasserena il ciglio	
Scena IV: Tirsi, e poi Clori Aria Tirsi: Se del tuo merito	Scena 3: Tirsi, e poi Clori Aria Tirsi: L'amor fortunato
Scena V: Clori sola Aria: Penerò: ma sola in pena	Scena 4: Clori sola Aria: Piango sì, ma non vogl'io
Scenery change: Ombrosa valle. . .	Scenery change: Ombrosa valle. . .
Scena VI: Fileno e poi Clori	Scena 5: Fileno e poi Clori
Scena VII: Fileno e poi Nice	Scena 6: Nice, e detti Aria Fileno: Fremo d'orror, di sdegno
Scena VIII: Nice, e poi Tirsi Aria Nice: Lasciami ingrato	Scena 7: Nice e Clori Aria clori: Vado lieta di mia sorte
Scena IX: Tirsi solo Aria: Mai, Ben mio, de' lacei suoi	Scena 8: Nice e poi Tirsi Aria Tirsi: Parto. Ma un sguardo solo
Fine dell'Atto Secondo	Scena 9: Nice sola Aria: Vorrei punir l'indegno
	Fine dell'Atto Secondo

c1748	c1754
Atto III	**Atto III**
Scena I: Nice e Clori Aria Nice: Ti lascio un core infido	Scena 1: Fileno e Nice
Scena II: Clori e poi Tirsi Aria Tirsi: Ritorno in vita	Scena 2: Tirsi e detti Aria Fileno: Vanne alla tua diletta
Scena III: Clori e poi Fileno Aria Fileno: T'ascolterei spergiura	Scena 3: Tirsi e Nice Aria Nice: Vederti ancor vogl'io
Scena IV: Clori sola Aria: Non pavento nel cimento	Scena 4: Tirsi solo Aria Tirsi: Mi rendo stupido
Scena V: Scenery change: Nice, e Fileno	Scena 5: Clori e Nice
Scena VI: Nice, e poi Tirsi. Fileno in disparte Aria Nice: Anima senza fe!	Scena 6 Clori sola Aria: Ho già penato assai
Scena Ultima: Tirsi, poi Clori. Fileno in disparte a sinistra indi Nice in disparte a destra. [Quartetto]	Scena 7: Sscenery change) Nice, e poi Fileno
Fine.	Scena Ultima: Tirsi col dardo e Clori. [poi Nice, poi Fileno] Duet: Tirsi and Nice: T: Ah! Mai più bell'idolo mio/non far torto della mia fè; N: Non temer. Già tua son io./ Troppo già penai per te Chorus (SATB)
Licenza	Fine del Dramma

Even beyond these basic differences, the two versions read differently. *T1748* reads more like a novel and less like an opera. Its recitative passages, in comparison to *T1754*, are long, often spanning a page or more in length.

In the opening scene complex of *T1748*, the shepherdess Clori has a soliloquy in which she relates her past actions (leaving Tirsi for Fileno) the actions of other characters (Nice and Tirsi have fallen in love) and her present state of mind (jealousy).

> Fra queste selve alfine
>
> Pur respirare in libertà poss'io.
>
> Chi vide mai del mio
>
> destin più capriccioso. Io per Fileno
>
> Tirsi abbandono, ed or che Tirsi acceso
>
> È per Nice d'amore,
>
> pace io non ho. Se il mio primiero affetto
>
> Mi si risvegli in petto,
>
> se m'agiti il pensiero
>
> Rivalità d'impero,
>
> Dir non saprei: Ma sia l'antica face:
>
> Sia dispetto novello io non ho pace.[76]

Her thoughts are interrupted by Fileno's entrance. His appearance and their subsequent conversation serve as an opportunity for Clori to display her true nature, which is that of a heartless liar. At first she tells Fileno to leave her alone. When he will not comply and instead gives all due protestations of love, Clori tries another tactic. She claims to have had a dream which filled her with fear: that her shepherd was in love with another. Fileno is now given the opportunity to reassure her

---

76 In this wood at last/ I am able to breathe freely./ Who could have foreseen/ my capricious fate? I, for Fileno left Tirsi,/ and now that Tirsi is / in love with Nice, / I have no peace. If my first affection/reawakens in my breast,/ it activates such thoughts/ of rivalry/ I cannot say: but be it my old flame,/ or be it a new annoyance I have no peace.

of his faithful love, not just through recitative, but by singing an aria to that effect.

> Come un sogno menzognero
> Può turbarti a questo segno?
> Hai pur teco, o cara, il pegno
> Del mio cor, che vive in te?
>
> Ei dirà, quant'é sincero
> Quell'amor, che a te giurai.
> Ei dirà, che non vedrai
> della mia più bella fe.[77]

This serves as his exit aria, but Clori is needed on stage to put her plans into action. Thus it is not until after Nice, the heroine of the drama, appears in Scene Two, and she and Clori converse that Clori can have her exit aria. Having lied to Fileno, she now falsely tells Nice that Tirsi has been swearing his love to every nymph in Arcadia.[78] Seeing Nice's shock, Clori then sings as if to reassure her:

> Non temer. Fedel se vuoi
> Solo a te sarà quel core.
> Son maestri i Lumi tuoi
> Di constanza, e fedeltà.
> Troppo vano è il tuo timore:
> Troppo ingiusto è il tuo sospetto.
> Chi potrà cangiar d'affetto,

---

77 How a lying dream/ is able to disturb you so much?/ Have you within thee, oh dear one, the pledge/ of my heart, that lives in [for) you?/ It will tell you, how sincere is/ that love, that is sworn to you./ It will tell you, that you cannot see/ a more beautiful faith than mine.

78 The terms "nymph" and "shepherdess" are used interchangeably to refer to the female inhabitants of Arcadia.

Se mirò la tua Beltà.[79]

Now she departs the stage. Tirsi then joins Nice in Scene Three. Here Nice accuses Tirsi of disloyalty and sings before parting:

Offri a più vaghi rai

Tutto quel core in dono.

Te conservar non sai.

Tutto quel cor per me.

Lasciami. Ti perdono:

Ma parlami sincero:

Ti soffrirò leggiero,

Non mancator di fe.[80]

Left alone for Scene Four, Tirsi wonders aloud how Nice could think him unfaithful, when he is completely in love with her:

Ah! Se il mio Bene è solo

De' miei pensieri il nido

Come mi trove infido

Fra i labbri del mio Ben.

V'è qualche trama ascosa?

È d'altri, è suo l'inganno?

Saria minor l'affanno

S'io l'intendessi almen.[81]

---

79 Do not fear./ That heart will be faithful only to you/ Your eyes are masters of/ constancy and faithfulness./ Too vain is your fear/ completely unjust is your suspicion/ who can change their feelings/ once he's seen your beauty.

80 You offer to prettier eyes/ all the gifts of (your) heart/and don't know how to preserve/ all that heart for me./ Leave me. I pardon you:/ but speak to me sincerely: I suffer you lightly, since I am not lacking in loyalty.

81 Ah! If my Dearest is/ the only shelter for my cares/ how am I found unfaithful/ by the lips of my Dearest/ Is there any secret intrigue/ is it from another, is it his lie?/ My pain would be less/ if I were to understand it at least.

The first scene of *T1754*, in contrast, opens with Clori and Nice. As in the other version, Clori relates her past actions and present plans:

In libertà quì almeno
Le mie pene sfogar posso una volta.
Chi vide mai del mio
Più stravagante umor? Tirsi che tanto
M'amò fedele, ingrata
Io per Filen lasciai. Giunge staraniera
Nice in Arcadia, ed or che acceso io miro
Tirsi d'amor per lei, fremo e sospiro.
Ma viene la rival. Mie frodi all'opra.
Di Tirsi a lei sospetta
Io renderò la fè. Mercè s'ei chiede
A' suoi novelli ardori
Da Nice in van, sarà ritorno a Clori.[82]

Unlike in *T1748*, however, in these thirteen lines appear the plot of the entire opera. Gone is the repetition of text. Clori is the catalyst for every character's subsequent actions. Nice appears immediately after this opening statement from Clori. Gone is the scene between Clori and Fileno, and therefore Fileno's first aria. Instead, the action moves along swiftly as Clori lies to Nice, sings an aria and exits the scene. Clori's first aria has some of the same imagery as the original, though its language is different:

---

82 In freedom here at least/ my pains lift for once./ who has never seen anything like/ my change of mood? / Tirsi who loved me too deeply/ I, for Fileno, in Arcadia as a stranger, and now that I see/ Tirsi loves her, trembles and sighs for her./ But here comes my rival. Into action with my deception./ I will make Tirsi's faithfulness suspect to her./ Hopefully when he seeks/ love from Nice in vain, he'll return to Clori.

Si sperar tu sola puoi

Di costringere quel core

A imparar dagli occhi tuoi

À serbar la fedeltà.

Scaddia pure dal tuo petto

Questo inutile timore.

Non potrà cangiar l'affetto

Nel mirar la tua beltà.[83]

With Tirsi's entrance, Scene Two begins. Nice immediately accuses him of disloyalty. She tells Tirsi to leave her and think about what he's done, although he protests his innocence through recitative and in an aria before leaving. His aria is now addressed to Nice:

Che vuoi ch'io pensi?

Io che t'adoro.

Che per te moro.

Ne'di te mai

Mi scorderò.

Credi a quei sensi

Figli del core.

Fido in amore

A tuoi bei rai

Sempre sarò[84]

---

83 If you hope only to be able/ to hold that heart/ to learn by your eyes/ to preserve loyalty/ Remove from your breast/ this useless fear./ It cannot change the feeling/ in the gaze of your beauty.

84 What do you want that I should think?/ I who adore you. /Who would die for you./ I will never forget about you./ Believe those senses/ daughters of the heart/ loyal in love/ to your beautiful eyes/ I will always be.

He then departs and Nice is left alone for Scene Three. Nice reveals her troubled state of mind, torn as she is between her hope that her faithful love is returned and her fear that Tirsi is simply a really good liar:

Ah! Per mia pace oh Dio!

Fido sperar vorrei

L'amato idolo mio

che degli affetti miei.

È ɩʼunico pensier.

Ma nel mio petto io sento

Voce, che dice al core

Per tu crudel tormento

Tu adori un traditore,

Un empio, un menzogner.[85]

From this discussion of the opening scenes, one already senses their different approaches to dramatic writing. *T1754* is much more concise in its use of characters. It also introduces the heroine and the villain at the opening of the drama. It gives them equal time on stage in terms of action and spoken dialogue.

The opening scene complex begins with Clori and ends with Nice, already thereby giving progression to the drama. Tirsi, the third most important figure in this triangle occupies the mid-point here. This opening has no scene equivalent to the first scene of *T1748*. Instead, the action and dialogue of that version are compressed in the later version.

---

85 Ah! For my peace, oh God!/ Loyal I hope will be/ my beloved idol/ that in my affec-tions/ is my only thought./ But in my breast I hear/ a voice, that says to my heart/ for your cruel torment/ you love a traitor/ a wicked one, a liar.

Note also the difference in poetic meter that exists in the aria texts of *T1754* compared to those of *T1748*. Although the music to the latter is no longer extant, this greater rhythmic variety in the poetry already would enhance the audience's interest in the drama.

Act Two in both operas takes place in a "shadowy wood." This type of scenery change was often used as a visual cue that dark misdeeds were about to be perpetrated on stage. *T1748* Maria Antonia gave Fileno several opportunities to sing "simple" songs such as this one-stanza aria which comes at the end of a monologue filled with troubling thoughts in Act II, Scene VI:

> Aure amiche, amico rio
> Col soave mormorio
> Consolate il mio dolor.[86]

Also missing from *T1754* are exchanges that could possibly be seen as comic even though they lend musical variety, such as this from Act II, Scene VII of *T1748*:

Nic: Dove o Filen?

Fil: Tirsi vedesti?

Nic: Al fonte
      con Clori, or lo lasciai.

Fil: Vendetta.

Nic: Ascolta,
      Ma Clori che ti fece?
      Qual motivo diè Tirsi a tuoi furori?

Fil: Un'infedele e Clori:
      E Tirsi un traditor.
      Io non ho calma in seno,

---

86 Gentle breezes, true friend/ with gentle murmuring/ console my sorrow.

> Se il barbaro non sveno,
>
> Se non punisco il perfido,
>
> Se non gli passo il cor.

Nic: Ma Pastor per pietà spiegati almeno: quai confuse querele. . .

Fil: È Clori un'infedele:

> È Tirsi un traditor?
>
> Voglio punir quel perfido,
>
> Voglio passargli il cor?

Nic: Forse ingannato eccedi,

Fil: Semplice! Prendi, e vedi

> Di, ch'io m'inganno ancor?[87]

In the *seria* style as championed by Metastasio and others, such commonplace dialogue had no place in the drama. The actions of all the characters are serious. Perhaps some wit is allowed, but the elegant shepherds and nymphs of *T1754* handle their excitement in more restrained tones.

---

87   Nic: Where to, o Fileno?

           Fil: Tirsi—have you seen him?

           Nic: At the fountain,

                    I left him there with Clori.

           Fil: Caught [in the act]!

           Nic: Listen,

                    but Clori what did she do to you?

                    What part does Tirsi have in your anger?

           Fil: An unfaithful one is Clori

                    And Tirsi a traitor.

                    I have no calm in my breast

                    if the savage does not bleed,

                    if the wicked one is not punished

                    if his heart is not pierced

           Nic: But, Shepherd, for mercy's sake, explain at least: this

                    confusing complaint. . .

           Fil: Is Clori unfaithful?

                    Is Tirsi a traitor?

                    Do I want to punish this wickedness?

                    Do I want to pierce the heart?

           Nic: Perhaps you are deceived and excede in your anger,

           Fil: Of course! Come and see

                    then, if I am still lying to myself.

The final act is revised in *T1754* as much as the other two. The basic action in each is as follows: Tirsi holds the dagger he had once given Clori as a token of affection. Clori had shown it to Fileno and Nice in Act II, claiming that Tirsi had just given it to her. In both versions, Nice and Fileno are eavesdropping on Tirsi as he stands baffled by the appearance of this long-forgotten object and by Nice's accusations of disloyalty. Clori appears to declare her love for Tirsi once and for all. He rejects her; Fileno and Nice appear from behind the bushes to celebrate his loyalty, and Clori is disgraced.

In *T1748*, Nice and Fileno are given interjections that distract the audience from the tension needed to build towards the final denouement. The stage directions are used to direct the actor/singers in revealing a character's feelings: Nice calls Clori "Amica" but "con ironia" (with irony). In a final break with verisimilitude, all four characters remain on stage, each with two verses to sum up his or her fate:

> Nic: Ah mio Tirsi or son felice:
>
> > Ma quel cor si cangierà?
>
> Tir: Tu il mio core ognor di Nice,
>
> > E di Nice ogn'or sarà.
>
> Clo: Ah Filen, tu sei sdegnato:
>
> > Ma quel cor di placherà?
>
> Fil: Il mio cor si sarà grato
>
> > Di trovar si in libertà.[88]

---

88   Nic: Ah my Tirsi now I am happy:
           but will that (your) heart change itself?
      Tir: My heart is now Nice's,
           and Nice's always will be.
      Clo: Ah Fileno you are disdained:
           but will that heart be placated?
      Fil: My heart will be so grateful
           to find itself free.

Then, as a four-person "chorus", they sing:

> Nic: Che contento!
>
> Clo: Che tormento!
>
> Tir & Fil: Che vicende fortunate!
>
> a 4: Nel mio caro à Voi, che amate
>
>   Imparate— Fedeltà.[89]

This is followed by a Licenza, an interpolated aria, which makes it clear that this opera was dedicated to Friedrich August, and that the loyalty sung about was not just of love between shepherds and nymphs, but that of a daughter (Maria Antonia as Nice) to a father and King.

In *T1754*, it is language more than acting ability which reveals the characters motivations and emotions. Stage directions are superfluous, since one knows from the poetry the irony of the situation or a character's statement. Clori reveals her treachery while trying to claim Tirsi for her own. She lies to him, claiming that Nice has left Arcadia. His responses to her reveal his innocence and his devotion to Nice. He declares he will find her, explain everything, and die for her if need be. These declarations are enough to convince Nice of the truth. She emerges from hiding to show Tirsi that she has heard everything and that she believes him. Clori tries one last act of treachery: trying to convince Fileno of her love. But he has heard the truth, and she can find no solace in his arms. Rather than comfort her, he leaves the stage. Her true character discovered, friendless and loveless, Clori knows she has been defeated by her own deeds, and she leaves the stage. Tirsi and Nice are left alone to celebrate their love in a duet.

---

89   Nic: What happiness!
      Clo: What torment!
      Tir & Fil: What a turn of events!
      a 4: In my dear o You that love
          Learn—Fidelity.

Tir: Ah mai più, bell Idol mio

    Non far torto alla mia fè.

Nic: Non temer. Già tua son io:

    Troppo già penai per te.

Tir: Mia tu sei?

Nic: Tu sei costante?

a 2: Non si trova un core amante

    Fortunato al par di me.

    Son contenti anch' i tormenti,

    Quando questa è la mercè.[90]

The world of Arcadia is kept through the end, even when a chorus of Nymphs and Shepherds joins the drama to celebrate Nice and Tirsi. No Licenza is to be found in this libretto, and verisimilitude is preserved.

In *T1748* the overriding concern seems to have been balancing stage time for each of the singers. In its opening scene complex, each character sings an aria. Each character has plenty of recitative. This is the pattern throughout. In each act, everyone has an aria, and each character has lots of recitative. The character of Fileno is more strongly drawn in this version than in *T1754*. A final count of the arias for each version reveals that there is much more balance among the characters in *T1748*: The heroine Nice has six, and everyone else has four. Adding a closing duet between Nice and Tirsi means that both the *prima donna* and the *primo uomo* have the largest share of the singing. In *T1754*,

---

90   Tir: Ah never more, beautiful Idol of mine
        Do not wrong my faith.
    Nic: Fear not. Already thine am I:
        Too much already have I pined for thee.
    Tir: Mine are you?
    Nic: Thou art constant?
    a 2: One does not find a loving heart
        As fortunate as I.
        Happy too are the torments,
        When this is the reward.

Clori has the largest number of arias (six), Nice has five, Tirsi has four and Fileno two. Combine this with the closing duet for Nice and Tirsi, and in *T1754*, Nice and Clori come away with equal aria time, Tirsi trails slightly, and Fileno is barely part of the drama.

Further examination of the libretti shows that in *T1748*, the villain Clori appears in a total of fourteen scenes to Nice's twelve. The situation is rectified in *T1754*, where Nice now appears in sixteen scenes compared with Clori's thirteen. Likewise, in *T1754*, Nice appears in the first scene together with Clori, giving this version dramatic tension from the outset.

Also, when counting arias, and considering that an aria is the most dramatic moment of any opera, and the place where a character gets to express her or his innermost thoughts, it is interesting that Nice does wind up with the lion's share of the arias in *T1748* (six vs Clori's four) as compared to *T1754* (five each for Clori and Nice). The shepherds Tirsi and Fileno are allotted four and three arias, respectively in *T1748* and five and three arias, respectively in *T1754*. If looked at from the view that the number of arias signals importance of the character, Nice wins clearly in the earliest *Trionfo* libretto, Clori and Tirsi are on equal footing and Fileno is the least important character. In the second *Trionfo*, Nice, Tirsi and Clori are put on equal footing, with Fileno again being of the least importance.

In each, there are only four scenes without an aria. But the action of *T1748* is made much more concise in *T1754*. There are instances throughout where the action that takes two or three scenes in *T1748* is condensed into one or two scenes in *T1754*. This is clearly the case between Scenes 1 and 5, as can be seen from my table, and occurs later in the opera as well. The language is made much more concise in the second libretto. What takes four scenes and four characters to explain in *T1748* needs only three scenes and two characters in *T1754*. Also, in order to heighten dramatic tension, a more gradual introduction of characters and ideas is visible in *T1754*. For example, Fileno does not appear on stage until Scene 5 in *T1754*. The overall structure of the opera remains the same in that Act I introduces the conflict, Act II heightens it, and Act III resolves it happily, but it is accomplished in a more *seria* style than *T1748*.

One can also analyze the dramatic structure in terms of dominance of the opera by its characters. In *T1748*, Clori is the first figure to appear, and is in six scenes in that act. In Act II, she dominates the middle of the act, and in Act III she is in five out of seven scenes, including the very end. Nice appears in four scenes in Act I, including the final two of that act. She opens Act II, appearing again in four scenes, and in Act III she is in four scenes, again dominating the end of the act.

Tirsi dominates the middle of the first act in which he appears four times. He likewise appears four times in the second act, mostly in scenes with Nice, but in Act III, he appears only three times, which is out of proportion to his importance in the drama: he is about to kill himself because Nice, believing him unfaithful, refuses to see him.

In this earliest version, Fileno is the character who seems to appear in more scenes than is necessary to his role in the drama: that of helper to the heroine. He appears in the opening of the entire drama (and in four scenes of the first act, equal number to Tirsi), the opening of the second act (though only in two scenes), and in the end of the third act (in an equal number of scenes to Tirsi: three). At the end, all characters stay on stage, each singing a line commensurate with their fate. But by this point in the drama, the characters become more like spokespeople for Maria Antonia in their praise of the King.

Comparing this to *T1754*, the drama is much clearer in terms of dramatic and musical progression. Act I is Clori's act, Act II is Nice's, and Act III is Tirsi's. This is made evident by the placement of the main arias and scenes: Clori opens and closes Act I; Nice opens and closes Act II; Tirsi appears at the beginning to Act II and has major arias in it; Nice opens and closes Act III; Tirsi's major dramatic moment (dagger at his breast) occurs in Act III and he and Nice close the act without Fileno and Clori, surrounded by a celebrating chorus of nymphs and shepherds whose singing closes the opera.

A comparison of the endings of *T1748* and *T1754* shows that in the latter, the ending is heightened dramatically, and has the advantage of removing the villain from the stage. It keeps the characters in their world of Arcadia instead of bringing them into the real world to praise the King. This is an important step in moving Maria Antonia's opera from the world of the court and into the public sphere.

The changes in the libretto stem from differing conceptions of audience: *T1754* is a pared-down version of the original, and in many ways reads like an opera intended for a public, not private, audience. For example, the librettist's transference of devotion to the King (*T1748*) to devotion to spouse and conjugal happiness (*T1754*) could signal a performance for one's peers, as the Arcadians were. The audience would consider the beauty of the poetry and its delivery paramount.[91] Amongst Arcadians, Her Highness' opera would be understood as affirming their highest poetic ideals. Furthermore, as a published work, a general audience outside the court would find the second version more appealing.

Maria Antonia's female characters are central to the drama, overshadowing their male counterparts. It is the shepherdess Nice who ultimately decides who lives and who dies in this opera. Her forgiveness of Tirsi creates the happy ending.

This is not an opera of gods against humans. It is on a smaller,

---

91   Tosi, pp 66-78 "On Recitative."

personal scale. In this way, Maria Antonia was of the times or indeed, foreshadowing a time when the nobility, like the general public would turn away from public spectacle and search for a drama that had closer ties to their lives and struggles. This is a disguised courtly life, where love is endangered by suspicion and jealousy.

The dramatic implications of the title are borne out in the characters: all are faithful to one another except Clori. Nice's character is the most varied. She sings of love, vengeance, faithfulness, and doubt. She is loving even when she rages. Tirsi, her faithful, though perpetually dumbfounded, suitor is either in love or lamenting the possible loss of it. Fileno, limited to two arias, is limited to expressing only two emotions: faithfulness in his first, anger in his second. Clori, though having many arias, likewise expresses only two emotions: glee and sadness. As if to emphasize this character's inability to deal with weightier emotions, the composer has given her only one aria that deals with sadness.

Is Nice Maria Antonia, and is Tirsi Friedrich Christian? There is no doubt that Maria Antonia took some of the inspiration for the main characters from her life, as do all artists. The love letters between the Princess and her Prince are full of the declarations of fidelity that are reminiscent of dialog from many a pastoral drama. Also, given that Friedrich Christian's secret name for himself was "Constant," it is just possible that the fidelity spoken of in the title refers to him.[92] It would seem that Maria Antonia is indicating just that in the quote that begins this chapter—that the characters were "close to the truth." The quote shows us that Maria Antonia saw herself and those around her reflected in her opera. Although much excellent work by women's history scholars cautions us against reading autobiographical content

92 See Schlechte, *Tagebuch*. A series of letters in HStA from a "Constant" may be love letters from Friedrich Christian to Maria Antonia, although they are (mis)filed under "Letters from Women."

into women's works, it seems that Maria Antonia expected and received just this sort of perception.

Musical Structure of *Trionfo*: The Librettist as Composer[93]

It is hard to determine which came first, the poetry or the music. From Maria Antonia's comments to Brühl, one might be right in assuming that, at least in part, she conceived of the music and poetry together. Thus, when Metastasio took the words without considering the music, this alone upset the structure of Maria Antonia's work. This meant starting from scratch if she wanted to have a coherent musical structure. Or did it?

There is evidence in the poetry to suggest that, at least in some cases, Maria Antonia re-used music from *T1748* with new texts. Take, for example, Clori's Act II, Scene V aria "Penerò: ma sola in pena"[94] from *T1748*, and the Act II, Scene 4 aria "Piango si, ma non vogl'io"[95] from *T1754*. The rhythm of the poetry in the latter is nearly identical to that of the earlier aria:

---

93 A comparison of Maria Antonia's style with that of Hasse, Porpora and Porta can be found in Drewes.

94 I will suffer: but alone in sorrow/ Shall not this soul meanwhile be./ I will weep: but alone to weeping/ This brow shall not be./ At least make another's sorrow/ My lot more serene:/ If appease love cannot,/ Vengeance shall appease.

95 I weep yes; but I don't want/ To live alone without hope;/ I shall enjoy at last, or together with me/ Will weep someone else yet./ There is no path that my fire/ That my heart will not undertake;/ So that vain love may be made/ Between the Nymph, and the Shepherd.

Penerò: ma sola in pena	Piango si; ma non voglio
Non sarà quest'alma intanto.	viver sola senza speme;
Piangerò: Ma solo al pianto	godrò alfine, o meco insieme
Questo ciglio non sarà.	piangerà qualch'altro ancor.
Renda almen l'altrui dolore	Via non v'è che il foco mio
La mia sorte più serena:	che il mio cor non intraprenda;
se appagar non può l'amore,	perchè vano amor si renda
La vendetta appagherà.	fra la Ninfa, ed il Pastor.

Although the music to *Trionfo 1748* is no longer extant, other musical differences are noticeable in the libretto: There is no chorus listed on the title page of *T1748*, but one appears in *T1754*. As Harris points out, by the early 18th century, the chorus was no longer a standard part of a pastoral drama, so it would seem that *T1748* harkens back to these older models. Also, not having a chorus is in keeping with a chamber work that would be conducted in a chamber setting. The chorus of *T1754* provides a musical summing up.

As written, neither libretto includes dances, which is typical of 18th-century Italian opera. Both versions break the fourth wall at the end, *T1748* with a concluding chorus of soloists, *T1754* with a chorus of nymphs and shepherds. Although no names are listed in either libretto, one could surmise that this opera was performed by Maria Antonia and other nobles, not professional singers, as would be the 1763 production of her second opera *Talestri*.[96]

An overarching tonal plan to the opera is apparent from the keys of individual arias. The orchestra and chorus serve as bookends to the

---

96 D: Dla, Loc. 382 Hoftheater, Ital. Oper, Ausgaben 1753-56, 1763ff. Even though the role of Tirsi is written using soprano clef, it is also possible that the role was sung an octave lower and by a tenor.

opera, starting with joy and ending with joy. The opening Sinfonia in D is in three movements, and instead of moving to the dominant for the second movement, the music moves instead to the subdominant. This middle movement makes use of a reduced texture: flutes and strings plus continuo.

The music then returns to the tonic and to full orchestra for the third movement. The dominant first appears in Clori's opening aria. Tirsi's first aria, "Che vuoi ch'io pensi," is in the subdominant, and his second aria, "Dille che fido io sono," is in the tonic; both are keys associated with the opening sinfonia. Fileno's first aria, "Come il misero augelletto," is about love and longing. He is singing about being far from his beloved, and the choice of B-flat makes this aria as far tonally as one can go from the key of A, which is Clori's opening key. Tirsi's Act III lament, "Mi rende stupido l'aspro dolore" is in E-flat which is as far away from D major as one can go within the tonal system. Thus the poor shepherd is far from his usual self. Each act ends with an aria in C except the third. If Clori had her way, perhaps this act would end in C, but since her plans are thwarted, the closing duet gloriously resounds in the dominant which leads nicely to the tonic for the closing chorus.

The orchestra consists of horns, oboes (often doubling violins), flutes (often doubling violins), violins 1 & 2, viola, and bass. There is little figured bass in the work, though this does not preclude the existence of a harpsichord or two in the orchestra. The main accompaniment for the arias is four-part strings. There are six instances of special instrumentation in the opera: Flutes are the instrument of choice in Act 1; horns appear in arias in Acts II and III; the special sound of muted strings appears in Act II and an obbligato oboe accompanies a different aria in Act 11.[97]

---

97 This last is also the only extant music notation in Maria Antonia's hand.

In the score as printed by Breitkopf, the characters share similar ranges and tessituras. Nice, Tirsi, and Clori are sopranos, Fileno is an alto. That said, there is not a great deal of difference in their vocal ranges, as can be seen from the table below.

Tessitura vs. Range

Aria	Range	Tessitura
Atto I		
Clori: Si sperar	e'-a"	g'-e'
Tirsi: Che vuoi	a-e"	g'-d"
Nice: Ah! Per mia pace	d'-a"	b'-g"
Tirsi: Dille	d'-f"	e'-b'
Fileno: Come il misero augelletto	c'-e"	d'-a'
Nice: Amalo pur se vuoi	d'-f"	g'-d"
Clori: Veder parmi già il mio bene	d'-g"	b'-f"
Atto II		
Nice: Serba per me fedele	e'-a-flat"	g'-g"
Tirsi: L'amor fortunato	c'-g"	g'-d"
Clori: Piango si, ma non vogl'io	e'-g"	b'-g"
Fileno: Fremo d'orror, di sdegno	a-d"	f'-c"
Clori: Vado lieta di mia sorte	d'-g"	g'-e"
Tirsi: Parto. Ma un sguardo solo	c'-f"	f'-d"
Nice: Vorrei punir l'indegno	d'-a"	b'-f"
Atto III		
Fileno: Vanne alla tua diletta	b-e"	f'-c"
Nice: Vederti ancor vogl'io	c#'-a"	e'-b'
Tirsi: Mi rendo stupido	a-d"	e'-b'
Clori: Ho già penato assai	d#'-a"	a'-e"
Nice and Tirsi: Ah! Mai più, bell' idol mio.	N: e'-f#"	N: g'-d"
	T:c'-e"	T: e'-b'

In addition, there is an aria (B-flat, voice + four-part strings & continuo) for Fileno "Lontan dagli occhi tuoi/io sempre vivo in pene/ senza mio bene, /pace per me non v'e" at the end of the Breitkopf publication. The score indicates that, if desired, this aria can replace Fileno's Act I aria.

What distinguishes these characters is not necessarily the instrumentation, but the mood of their utterances. The most limited character in this is Fileno. He has two arias and no act-closing accompanied recitative. His two emotions are loving devotion and rage. His recitatives allow him to become a slightly more fully developed character.

To show that Nice and Tirsi are meant for one another, the recitatives between them highlight their similarity. A great example comes from Act II, Scene Two: whenever one ends a phrase, often the other begins their phrase on the same note (Illustration 6.1; see bracketed part of middle system).

Illustration 6.1: *Trionfo 1754*, Act II, Scene II, Nice and Tirsi's Recitative

At first, it is Tirsi who picks up on Nice's tones (mm. 12, 17), then Nice begins to do so (mm. 29). She follows this by echoing his cadential formulae (mm. 53-56). An extended session of beginning on the previous end note follows (mm. 58-65). This text setting is perfectly in keeping with the objectives of the two characters at this point: Tirsi is declaring his love for Nice. She wants no part of it, and thus avoids matching his notes until measure 29, where she changes tactics by interrupting Tirsi, and moving the music to a cadence herself. They argue, Tirsi begins to leave. Nice stops him by echoing his cadences. And when they again argue about whether Tirsi should leave or stay, they again share notes. Similar musical devices are used in recitatives between Fileno and Clori (see Illustration 6.2): Fileno ends on f', Clori begins her phrase on f' and so on. Here, however, Clori is lying to Fileno.

Illustration 6.2: *Trionfo 1754*, Act II, Scene V, Clori and Fileno's Recitative

Even though the aria total in *T1754* is higher than that in *T1748* (eighteen compared to seventeen), the importance of the characters to the creation of the drama cannot come from an aria and scene count alone. One needs to look at the types of arias, and the ways in which a composer achieves musical variety within the work. Gone are the "simple songs" of previous pastoral dramas. *T1754* is a pastoral drama in the *seria* style, and as such, all of its arias are *da capo* or *dal segno*. This would seem to imply a great deal of similarity from beginning to end, but in reality, the arias are varied by tempo, instrumentation, and dynamics that make the music engaging from beginning to end.

Chapter 7

Her Highness' Voice

What little we know of Maria Antonia as a singer comes from the observations of others. The most well known of these was Burney's observation, made in 1773, that "She sung in a truly fine style; her voice is very weak, but she never forces it, or sings out of tune. She spoke the recitative, which was an accompanied one, very well in the way of great old singers of better times."[98] This report was made close to the end of Maria Antonia's life, after she had given birth to several children, and had had many bouts of severe illness. It is therefore not surprising that her voice would be weak at this point in her life.

Reports from Graf Wackerbarth inform us of Her Highness' singing abilities and, more importantly, what was expected of her: from a letter dated 13 Nov 1748, "Madame the Electoral Princess sang yesterday evening with admirable taste the Cantata [her *Didone Abbandonata*], of which I have the honor of enclosing a copy."[99] No matter what she

---

98 Burney, p. 51.
99 "Madame la Princesse E^le chanta hier au soir avec un gout admirable la Cantata, dont j'ai l'honneur de joindre ici copie." Letter to Graf Brühl, à Dresde ce 13 Nov 1748.

created, as long as it was done with good taste, upholding the propriety of her station, then it was acceptable and pleasing to her audience.

Obviously, the best source for how Maria Antonia's compositional and vocal abilities reflect concepts of tastefulness remain the works composed by Her Highness herself. To start with, Maria Antonia was a soprano. As a singer, she had at her disposal the ability to sing heavily ornamented vocal lines. She was fond of lines that ascended by leap and then descended with stepwise motion, something already evident in the early arias discussed in Chapter 4. She had wonderful breath control, as evidenced by long roulades found in her music. A preference for the mid-high part of her vocal range (from a' to f") is also noticeable. Nice's final aria from Act II, "Vorrei punir l'indegno," will serve to illustrate how tastefulness governed her music.

The text is as follows:

Vorrei punir l'indegno
vorrei strappargli il core
ma mi trattiene amore
e sospirar mi fa.

M'avvampa in sen lo sdengo
ed hò sul ciglio il pianto,
ah ch'io vaneggio intanto
fra l'ira e la pietà.[100]

Maria Antonia spun an aria from four motives, each for one line of text from the opening quatrain (Illustrations 7.1a & b): an ascending octave (Vorrei punir l'indegno); a leap filled in with descending

---

100 I would like to punish the unworthy one/ I would like to tear out his heart/ but love restrains me/ and makes me sigh./ Disdain burns in my breast/ and I am up to my brow in tears/ ah! because I am tossed/ between anger and pity.
(Please note that the mixture of emotions that the word *pietà* conjures in Italian [mercy, pity, compassion, and piety] is hard to render with a single word in English.)

stepwise triplets (vorrei strappargli il core); a longer, more lyrical motif that essentially ornaments a single note (ma mi trattiene amore); and a descending, syncopated sixth (e sospirar mi fa). The motif for "e sospirar mi fa" is extended through ornamentation on its repetition (see Illustrations 7.1c and 7.1d). Furthermore, just as Nice vacillates between anger and pity, so the tempo of her music moves from fast (*Allegro*) to slow (*Adagio*) and back.

Illustration 7.1a: *Trionfo 1754*, Act II, Scene IX, "Vorrei punir l'ndegno" motives

Illustration 7.1b: *Trionfo 1754*, Act II, Scene IX, "Vorrei punir l'indegno" motives continued

Illustration 7.1c: "sospirar" motif

Illustration 7.1d: "sospirar" motif continued

As for instrumentation, the oboe—possibly the instrument that most resembles a human voice—is chosen to comment upon the emotions expressed by Nice through parallel thirds and sixths (see Illus. 7.1c, mm. 24-26), echoing her at m. 28, and then replacing her vocal melismas with its own melismas (Illus. 7.1d, mm. 31-34). The aria is in C major, the act-closing key. Tonally, the music moves from tonic to dominant and back to tonic for the A-section. Its B-section is in the relative minor, A minor.

The variations and cadenzas Maria Antonia created for this aria are further illustrations of her tastefulness (see Illustration 7.2). They are never placed too high in the voice and are not overly showy. They have a graceful and dignified quality which enhances the musical line and the emotional quality expressed by the character.

Illustration 7.2: *Variazione e cadenze dell'Aria a Oboe Solo,* excerpt

What her audience heard in this aria and throughout the opera is music rather conservative in style—all the arias are in *da capo* or *dal segno* form—but made contemporary through the use of internal metric, dynamic, and tempo shifts. This keeps the music interesting from beginning to end, even though it does not dispense with full ritornelli, or interrupt a character in mid-aria— techniques employed by composers such as Jomelli.

To compare Maria Antonia's music to that of professional composers such as Hasse and her poetry to that of Metastasio as Drewes, Yorke-Long, and others have done is to use the wrong yardstick. On such an international scale, she would not perhaps get the hearing she deserves. Composers competing for the public's attention, those who needed to earn their way in the world through their compositions, were much more likely to be bold, daring, and interested in standing out from the rest of the pack. Other composers needed no such compulsion to write. The approval of the aristocracy was its own reward, and being squarely in the center of the musical soundscape of the period was a great achievement. Composers such as Maria Antonia, Frederick II of Prussia, and Wilhelmine von Bayreuth need to be understood within this cultural context.

The Curious Case of the 1768 Vienna Libretto

Maria Antonia's pastoral was not simply a work for her own enjoyment. It found its way into print beyond Dresden. A version of *Trionfo* was performed in Vienna in 1768 and is only known to us from its libretto, a copy of which may be found in the Houghton Library at Harvard University. Only one other copy of this is known to exist, and this libretto is fascinating in its similarity and dissimilarity to both *T1748* and *T1754*.

For a start, nowhere on this libretto does Maria Antonia's name appear. Neither librettist nor composer are listed, although the cast members are. They are La Signora Antonia Bernasconi as Nice, Teresa Eberardi as Clori, Signore Emanuele Cornacchini as Tirsi, and Signor Filippo Laschi as Fileno (and listed here as "virtuoso di Camera di S. A. R. Il Principe Carlo Duca di Lorena di Baar &c. &c."). There is a chorus, and in addition, dances are a part of the drama, something not to be found in either of the earlier versions. No changes of scenery are noted, although many of the stage directions are kept. This work is, as it says on the cover page, being presented "per la prima volta ne' Teatri Privilegiati di Vienna." The printer for the libretto is Ghelen.

T1768 is more concise dramatically than either the 1748 or 1754 versions, and it has more musical variety. For example, the end of Act I in *T1748* had three scenes: Scene Eight featured Clori alone, Scene Nine featured Clori in conversation with Nice, and finishing that scene with an exit aria ("Tra fiori, e tra le fronde"), Scene Ten was Nice's alone, and she finished the act in grand style with her aria "Esci mio cor di pena." In *T1754*, this scene complex was trimmed to two scenes: first Clori and Nice with Nice singing an exit aria ("Amato pur se vuoi"), then Clori alone in Scene Eight hoping to celebrate her victory ("Veder parmi gia il mio bene"). *T1768* dispenses with these and instead gives Clori and Nice one scene together. The basic action is the same: Clori lies to Nice, saying that Tirsi has declared his affection for Clori; Nice then renounces Tirsi, telling Clori that she may love him if it pleases her, but that she (Nice) will have nothing to do with a traitor. Here, instead of two arias and multiple scenes, there is one page of recitative followed by a duet (Illustration 7.3).

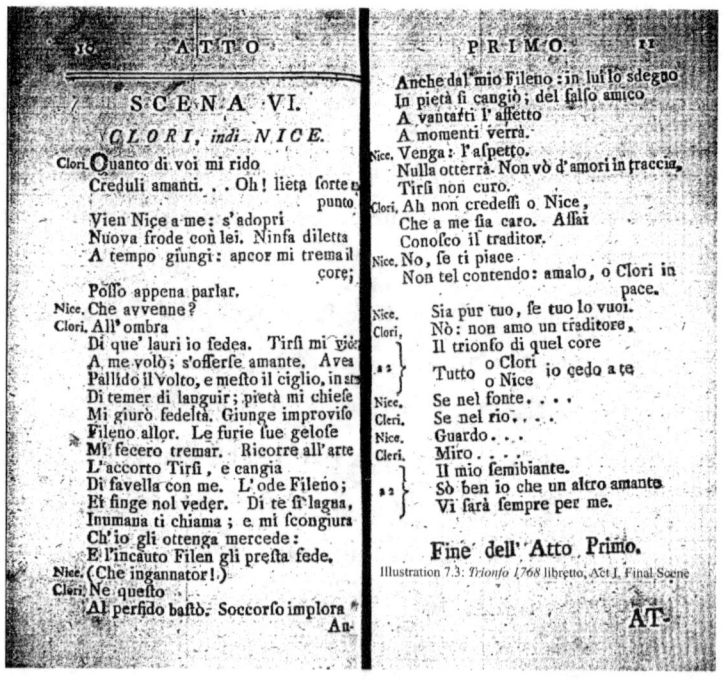

Illustration 7.3: *Trionfo* 1768 libretto, Act I, Final Scene

Throughout this version of *Trionfo* are numerous duets, as well as a terzetto. The metric variety in the poetry is more pronounced than in either of the two previous versions. For example, Tirsi's aria in Act Two, Scene One is broken into two parts. Each consists of six lines, and these are on either side of his opening recitative (Illustration 7.4).

Illustration 7.4: *Trionfo 1768*, Act II, Scene One

Furthermore, his aria opens the act, as does Nice's "Punir vorrei quel traditor" in Act III of this version. No longer are arias reserved for the end of a scene or act, nor do they provide a reason for the character to leave the stage. The concern for verisimilitude is perhaps greatest in this version of *Trionfo*. Some of these arias would seem to move away from the *da capo/dal segno* format such as the two just cited.

Tirsi's aria "Selve ombrose" actually serves a dual purpose: it expresses a mood and serves as shorthand for a scenery change (since Act II opens in a shadowy glade). The dialogue is more concise in *T1768* than in either of the two early versions. Although her aria count has shrunk, by her opening and closing both Acts I and II, Nice stands out further as the heroine. The character of Tirsi seems to have slightly more importance in this version than in the earlier ones, using the number of arias as an indication (five, compared to Nice's four; Clori and Fileno have two each).

Many of the arias here are the same as those in *T1754*. The first four are exactly the same. Nice's Act II, Scene Two aria from *T1754* "Serba per me fedel" is here, as is Clori's "Piango si" and Fileno's "Fremo d'orror". From Act III, only Fileno's "Vane alla tua diletta" and the final duet between Nice and Tirsi remain. The ending of this version gives more importance to Fileno who, in turn, lends a bit more dramatic realism to the work: it is he who brings out the chorus of "Ninfe e Pastori" (Nymphs and Shepherds) to celebrate the victory of fidelity, whereas in *T1754* the chorus had simply appeared, and in *T1748* there was no chorus except that of the four soloists.

Comparison of the Three Versions of *Il trionfo della fedeltà*		
c1748	c1754	1768
Atto Pmo [Primo]	**Atto I**	**Atto Primo**
Scena I: Clori e Fileno Aria Fileno: Come un sogno menzognero	Scena 1: Clori e Nice Aria Clori: Si sperar tu sola puoi	Scena 1: Clori e Nice Aria Clori: Si sperar tu sola puoi
Scena II: Clori e Nice Aria Clori: Non temer. Fedel se vuoi	Scena 2: Nice e Tirsi Aria Tirsi: Che vuoi ch'io pensi?	Scena II: Nice e Tirsi Aria Tirsi: Che vuoi ch'io pensi?
Scena III: Nice e Tirsi Aria Nice: Offri a più vaghi rai	Scena 3: Nice sola Aria: Ah! Per mia pace oh Dio!	Scena III: Nice sola Aria: Ah! Per mia pace oh Dio!
Scena IV: Tirsi solo Aria: Ah! Se il mio Bene è solo		
Change of scenery	Change of scenery	No change of scenery
Scena V: Fileno e poi Tirsi	Scena 4: Tirsi, e Fileno fra diversi parti	Scena IV: Fileno, poi Tirsi da diversi parti, indi Clori Aria Tirsi: Dille: che fido io sono

Scena VI: Clori e detti	Scena 5: Clori in disparte, e detti Aria Tirsi: Dille: che fido io sono	

Comparison of the Three Versions of *Il trionfo della fedeltà*		
c1748	c1754	1768
Atto Secondo	**Atto Secondo**	**Atto Secondo**
Scena I: Nice e Fileno	Scena 1: Nice, Fileno e poi Tirsi	Scena Prima: Tirsi, poi Fileno Two "simple" arias by Tirsi: Selve ombrose and Il Leggiadro tuo sembiante
Scena II: Tirsi e Detti	Scena 2: Tirsi e Nice Aria Nice: Serba per me fedele	Scena II: Fileno, poi Nice
Scena III: Tirsi e Nice Aria Nice: Ah rasserena il ciglio		Scena III: Tirsi e Nice Aria Nice: Serba per me fedele
Scena IV: Tirsi, e poi Clori Aria Tirsi: Se del tuo merito	Scena 3: Tirsi, e poi Clori Aria Tirsi: L'amor fortunato	Scena IV: Tirsi, e poi Clori Aria Tirsi: Di questo cor è Nice
Scena V: Clori sola Aria: Penerò: ma sola in pena	Scena 4: Clori sola Aria: Piango sì, ma non vogl'io	Scena V: Clori sola Aria: Piango sì, ma non vogl'io
Scenery change: Ombrosa valle. . .	Scenery change: Ombrosa valle. . .	No scenery change
Scena VI: Fileno e poi Clori	Scena 5: Fileno e poi Clori	Scena VI: Fileno, e poi di nuovo Clori
Scena VII: Fileno e poi Nice	Scena 6: Nice, e detti Aria Fileno: Fremo d'orror, di sdegno	Scena VII: Nice, e detti Aria Fileno: Fremo d'orror, di sdegno

Scena VIII: Nice, e poi Tirsi Aria Nice: Lasciami ingrato	Scena 7: Nice e Clori Aria clori: Vado lieta di mia sorte	Scena VIII: Clori, e Nice
Scena IX: Tirsi solo Aria: Mai, Ben mio, de' lacei suoi	Scena 8: Nice e poi Tirsi Aria Tirsi: Parto. Ma un sguardo solo	Scena IX: Tirsi, e detti Terzetto (Tirsi, Nice, Clori): Partirò, Morirò
Fine dell'Atto Secondo	Scena 9: Nice sola Aria: Vorrei punir l'indegno	[Fine dell Atto Secondo]
	Fine dell'Atto Secondo	

Three Versions of *Il trionfo della fedeltà* Continued		
c1748	c1754	1768
Atto III	**Atto III**	**Atto Terzo**
Scena I: Nice e Clori Aria Nice: Ti lascio un core infido	Scena 1: Fileno e Nice	Scena I: Nice, indi Fileno, poi Tirsi "Simple" Aria Nice: Punir vorrei quel traditor (opens the act) Aria Fileno: Vanne alla tua diletta
Scena II: Clori e poi Tirsi Aria Tirsi: Ritorno in vita	Scena 2: Tirsi e detti Aria Fileno: Vanne alla tua diletta	
Scena III: Clori e poi Fileno Aria Fileno: T'ascolterei spergiura	Scena 3: Tirsi e Nice Aria Nice: Vederti ancor vogl'io	Scena II: Nice, e Tirsi Aria Nice: Non dir che m'ami
Scena IV: Clori sola Aria: Non pavento nel cimento	Scena 4: Tirsi solo Aria Tirsi: Mi rendo stupido	Scene [sic] III: Tirsi [solo] Aria Non so resistere al rio dolore
Scena V: Scenery change: Nice, e Fileno	Scena 5: Clori e Nice	Scena IV: Clori e Nice

Scena VI: Nice, e poi Tirsi. Fileno in disparte Aria Nice: Anima senza fe!	Scena 6 Clori sola Aria: Ho già penato assai	Scena V: Clori [sola] Aria: Mi posso insuperbir: Trionfo! Ho vinto!
Scena Ultima: Tirsi, poi Clori. Fileno in disparte a sinistra indi Nice in disparte a destra. [Quartetto]	Scena 7: Scenery change) Nice, e poi Fileno	Scena VI: Nice, e Fileno: dietro a lei frettoloso
Fine.	Scena Ultima: Tirsi col dardo e Clori. [poi Nice, poi Fileno] Duet: Tirsi and Nice: T: Ah! Mai più bell'idolo mio/non far torto della mia fè; N: Non temer. Già tua son io./Troppo già penai per te Chorus (SATB)	Scena VII: Tirsi, e Clori, poi Nice, poi Fileno a 2: Nice and Tirsi: Son contenti, anche i tormenti/ Quando questa è la mercè
Licenza	**Fine** del Dramma	Scena Ultima: Fileno conseguito di Ninfe e Pastori Chorus alternating with Fileno solo, duet Tileno and Tirsi, and trio Nice, Tirsi and Fileno.
		Fine

Summary of *Il trionfo della fedeltà* as published by Breitkopf, 1756				
Recitative	Aria	Mood	Tempo, Key, Meter, Type	Special Instruments
Atto I				
Scena I: Clori enters and explains how, though she was once Tirsi's beloved, she left him for Fileno. Explains that Tirsi now loves Nice, the new shepherdess in Arcadia. States how she will attempt to break apart this happy union at which point Clori expects Tirsi to return to her. Nice, seeking Tirsi and not knowing Clori, arrives on the scene. Clori lies, telling Nice to be careful, that Tirsi is unfaithful.	Clori: Si sperar	Mocking	Allegretto, A (B section in a), 3/8, Da Capo	

Scena II: Nice and Tirsi. Nice can't believe her ears. Accuses Tirsi of disloyalty. Tirsi cannot under-stand why she doubts his love.	Ah! Per mia pace	Love and foreboding	Largo e cantabile (B section Allegro), F (B section in d), 3/4, Da Capo	
Scena IV: Tirsi and Fileno. The former rivals for Clori's affections now declare themselves friends since Fileno is happily in love with Clori, and Tirsi is in love with Nice.				
Scena V: Clori on the side, and the others. Clori tells Tirsi that Nice doubts his love.	Tirsi: Dille che fido io sono	Love	Andante, D (B section in b), 3/4, Dal Segno	Flutes

Scena VI: Fileno and Clori. F: Your concern for Tirsi makes me wonder, Clori. C: I'm tired of your suspicions, Fileno. Do not doubt my love. F: I'm sorry my precious. C: Go, I forgive you. F: My dearest, until later.	Fileno: Come il misero augelletto	Love and longing	Andante (B section Allegretto), B flat (B section in g), 3/8, Dal Segno	
Scena VII: Clori and Nice. Clori claims to have been approached by Tirsi, and offered his love. Claims Fileno to be furiously jealous. Nice tells Clori that she will have nothing to do with someone so inconstant.	Nice: Amalo pur se vuoi (You can love him if you want, but I want nothing to do with that liar	Rage	Allegro (B section Andante), E (B section in e), 2/4 (in B section 3/8), Dal Segno	Flutes in B section.
Scena VIII: Clori celebrates her seeming victory.	Clori: Veder parmi già il mio bene	Joy and anticipation	Allegro con spirito, C (in B section a), Common Time, Dal Segno	

Atto II				
Scena I: Fileno and Nice, then Tirsi. Fileno tries to convince Nice of Tirsi's faithfulness. Tirsi enters and expresses his love for Nice, but she retains her doubts.				
Scena II: Nice accuses Tirsi of infidelity. Each doubts the other's love. Nice finishes by saying "if you are true to me, prove it."	Nice: Serba per me fedele (Remain faithful to me)	Hope tinged with doubt	Un poco Lento (in B section Andantino), E-flat (B section in c), Common Time (in B section 2/4), Da Capo	Horns
Scena III: Tirsi e poi Clori. Tirsi is now convinced that Nice loves him. He expresses his love for Nice and his joy to Clori, who despairs.	Tirsi: L'amor fortunato	Joyful love	Allegro, C (B section in a), 3/4, Da Capo	

Scena IV: Clori sola. Angry, she plots more treachery in order to win Tirsi for herself.	Piango si, ma non vogl'io	Sadness and anger	Un poco Lento (B section Allegro), g (B section in B flat), Common Time, Dal Segno	
Scena V: Fileno, e poi Clori. Clori shows Fileno a dagger that Tirsi had given her long ago (when she and Tirsi were lovers) as if it were a recent gift. Fileno believes Tirsi to be disloyal to Nice.				
Scena VI: Nice, e detti. Fileno shows Nice the dagger, upon which is an inscription of eternal love. Nice despairs. Fileno swears vengance on her behalf.	Fileno: Fremo d'orror, di sdegno	Rage	Allegro assai, F (B section in d), Common Time (for last half of B section 3/4), Da Capo	Horns

Scena VII: Nice e Clori. N: For you he has betrayed me and Fileno. C: Am I guilty if Tirsi loves me?	Clori: Vado lieta di mia sorte	Joy	Allegro ma non troppo (second half of B section Andantino), G (B section in e), Common Time (B section in 3/4), Da Capo	
Scena VIII: Nice e poi Tirsi. Nice prepares to leave Arcadia. Tirsi appears and tries to stop her. Swears his love. She tells him to leave her.	Tirsi: Parto. Ma un sguardo solo	Lamentation	Lento (B section Allegro), f (B section in A flat), Common Time, Dal Segno	Muted strings
Scena IX: Nice Sola. (Recitativo accompagnato) I'm leaving.	Vorrei punir l'indegno	Rage and compassion	Allegro and Adagio (B section Allegro), C (B section in a), Common Time, Dal Segno	Solo Oboe
Atto III				
Scena I: Fileno and Nice. F: Wait Nice, don't leave. Stay and let me avenge you.				

Scena II: Tirsi e detti. Fileno threatens to kill Tirsi with the dagger. Nice stops Fileno: I pardon his offense, and so I am already vindicated. Let him live. Tirsi attempts to plead his case. Fileno will not listen.	Fileno: Vanne alla tua diletta [Go to your delight]	Rage, disgust	Allegro ma non troppo, E (B section in c#), Common Time, Dal Segno	

Scena III: Tirsi and Nice: Tirsi does not understand what is happening. "What is my crime?" Nice responds, "Ask your heart." Tirsi says, "If I have offended you then here: here's the dagger, kill me." "No," says Nice. "Live ingrate. I leave you to your remorse. I no longer love you. Farewell."	Nice: Vederti ancor vogl'io [Live and remember how your treachery cost you love]	Indignation	Allegro assai (in B section Andantino), D (B section in d), 6/8 (in B section 2/4), Da Capo	Horns
Scena IV: Tirsi solo [Recitativo accompagnato directly into Aria] "I still do not know what I have done to lose my beloved and my friend. What heart can be as tormented as mine? I am dying of grief."	Mi rende stupido l'aspro dolore	Lamentation	Andante in B section Andantino), E-flat (B section in c), Common Time (in B section 3/4), Dal Segno	

Scena V: Clori and Nice. Nice declares her intention to leave Arcadia. Clori does not try to stop her.				
Scena VI: Clori sola. "I've won!"	Ho già penato assai	Joy	Allegro, C (B section in a), Da Capo	

Scena VII: Nice and then Fileno. Nice arrives too late to the river bank. The raging river has swept away the bridge. Fileno arrives and tells her that they were both mistaken. He encoun- tered Tirsi, pale, half-dead and threat- ening suicide unless Fileno would listen to him. Fileno listened and Tirsi explained that he was still loyal to Nice. F and N decide to eavesdrop upon a conversation between Tirsi and Clori.				

Scena Ultima: Nice and Fileno overhear Clori explaining to Tirsi how she plotted to win him back. Tirsi, despairing and hoping to win Nice back, says that he will go after her and explain everything, whether or not Nice believes him. At that moment, Nice comes from behind the bush and explains how she and Fileno have heard everything. Fileno rejects Clori, who leaves the stage, defeated. Nice and Tirsi celebrate their love.	Nice & Tirsi Duet: Ah! Mai più, bell'idol mio	Joyful love	Un poco Andante (in B section Allegretto), A (B section in a), Common Time (B section in 3/4), Da Capo	
Chorus of Nymphs and Shepherds	In piacer cangiate	Celebration	Allegro, D, 3/8, Through composed	Horns

The text of the closing chorus differs markedly from that of *T1754*. Instead of celebrating fidelity between both members of the happy couple, it celebrates Nice in conventional terms relating to female beauty:

T1754

In piacer cangiate i pianti
Fidi sposi, Fidi amanti!
Della frodi, e dell'inganno
Trionfò la fedeltà.
Benchè soffra ingiusto affanno
Mai non perda ancor speranza
L'un cor cede alla costanza
Del destin la crudeltà.[101]

T1768

Coro:
Celebriam, Ninfe, e pastori
Questa amabile Donzella,
La più fida, la più bella
Lo splendor di nostra età.
Frà festosi allegri Cori
Il bel nome adorni il Tempio.

Tirsi e Fileno: E si mostri per esempio / D'innocenza, e fedeltà

---

101 Into smiles change the tears/ Faithful spouses, Faithful lovers!/ over deception and lies/ triumphs fidelity!/ Although one suffers unjustly/ never lose hope/ that a heart will yield to constancy/ from a cruel destiny.

Coro:
Sparga Imeme, e sparga amore
Sulla coppia fortunata,
Ogni di gioja maggiore,
E maggior felicità.[102]

It is a different treatment, to be sure, and most likely not a version authorized by Maria Antonia. There is no information on how this came to be performed in Vienna. This pastoral would have been performed at a time when the court had tired of large public festivals and began to enjoy musical events that would require smaller forces and less expense. It is known that Maria Antonia sent copies of her operas to her imperial relatives in Vienna. A copy of *Trionfo* in the Austrian National Library bears a Dresden watermark and is in a hand similar to that associated with other Maria Antonia manuscripts. Emperor Franz Joseph owned the copy of *T1768* that is in the Austrian National Library. Unfortunately, as is the case at the Houghton Library, there is no extant copy of the music to this libretto.

This *Trionfo* appears to be an unauthorized revision of Maria Antonia's work, and it sheds light on the quote which opens Chapter 6. It indicates that she may have been cognizant of attempts to attribute her work to others. Therefore, through her publications, Maria Antonia was reclaiming her authorship of this work. How Maria Antonia dealt with issues of authorship is examined in my next chapter, along with her patronage of the arts outside of court.

---

102 Let us celebrate, Nymphs and shepherds/ this lovely maiden / the most faithful, the most beautiful /the splendor of our age. / Among festive joyous choirs / her beautiful name adorns the temple / [Tirsi & Fileno: And be shown by example /innocence and fidelity] / scatter Hymen, and scatter Love / on the fortunate couple / every great joy / and great happiness.

Chapter 8
The Princess and the Enlightenment

Toward the middle of the 1750s, Maria Antonia and Friedrich Christian begin to emerge as political and cultural figures in their own right. They were unofficially in command of the Residenzschloss in Dresden during those portions of the year when the King and Queen were in Poland. As such, it is possible that they had greater say in their public image than was evident from the 1751 court portraits. Illustration 8.1 is part of a series of portraits of the royal family by the principal court painter, Pietro Graf Rotari, which dates from 1754 (see next page).

Rotari portrays the Princess in practically bourgeois fashion. Her red dress, though accented with fur, is simple in its cut and its avoidance of oversized panniers. She wears a black lace collar around her neck, instead of elaborate jewelry, and the simple curled wig on her head could easily be her own powdered hair, decorated with a black flower decoration. The few signs of her status, in addition to the fur, are the white lace at the sleeves and breast of her dress and the diamond buttons down the front.

On the table in front of her is the libretto to her first opera, *Il trionfo della fedeltà*. She holds the title page in her right hand. Underneath this is the score to an aria, only the first words of which—"La clemenza e la pietà son te" ("Clemency and mercy are you")—are visible. Underneath this is a painter's brush, and a drawing of Minerva, the goddess of wisdom and protector of all the arts.

From this painting alone, we learn that Maria Antonia was seen, and wished to be seen, not only as a patron, but also as a creator of art. The portrait of her spouse likewise portrays him in a fashion that is not overly ceremonial, although it shows him with a breastplate, sword, and helmet. His jacket, though cuffed with ermine, is simple in its cut. His royal crest is practically out of view, and his hair is also simply styled. Maria Antonia and Friedrich Christian are dressed less like future absolutist rulers and more like good Saxon bourgeois citizens. You can view the portrait here: https://skd-online-collection.skd.museum/Details/Index/286064

As a patron of the arts, Maria Antonia could be confident that her public image would be a positive one. Women could, however, suffer a loss in public standing, with respect to performing in public. Maria Antonia was all too aware of this: her music and poetry remained in manuscript form for long periods. Her translation and adaptation of Psalm 53, the *Miserere* found its way into print under a pseudonym.

Il trionfo della fedeltà might have shared this fate or remained in manuscript but for two events: possible plagiarism and the interest in Italian culture of one of the most important couples of the time: Johann and Luise Gottsched.

Why Go Public?: Debates over Authorship

As was already discussed, Maria Antonia's creativity flourished in her new home. Following the success of her cantatas for the King and Queen, she went on to compose poetry based on classical themes. Maria Antonia performed her cantatas *Didone* and *Lavinia* in November 1748.[103] Through the Dresden court poet and fellow Arcadian Abbate Giovanni Claudio Pasquini,[104] Maria Antonia sent her libretto of *Trionfo* to Abbate Pietro Metastasio, court poet at the imperial court in Vienna, also an Arcadian.[105] The libretti to the cantatas *Lavinia* and *Nice* and her canzonetta *Didone* had already been sent to Metastasio. On 25 January 1749, he wrote to Pasquini praising these libretti in glowing terms. He said in part:

> I could never in eternity have imagined that a princess would come to write in poetry, and in a foreign language, with such excellence. In the two cantatas and the canzonetta it is not only admirable the delicate adjustment of thoughts, the connection of ideas, the nobility of phrase, the harmony of verse, and the chosen tenderness of expression; but what surprises me most is a certain artful ease, for which happy natural talents are not enough, but a firmness of wrist is supposed,

---

103 Wackerbarth to Brühl, 13 Novembre and 20 Novembre 1748.

104 Known among the Arcadians under the pseudonym Trigeno (or Tirgenio) Migonitidio.

105 His Arcadian pseudonym was Artino Corasio. A "Favola Pastorale" from him was sent to Metastasio at the end of 1747 (*Tutte le opere di Pietro Metastasio*, p. 333). This is possibly the earliest reference to *Trionfo*, but the sources remain unclear as to whether this was, indeed, a work by Pasquini or the opera by Maria Antonia sent under Pasquini's name.

which cannot be acquired except by long and assiduous practice. . .[106]

In a later letter, Metastasio refers to a later shipment of Maria Antonia's poetry with these words: "Oh poor us, dear Pasquini! If sovereigns write poetry of such excellence, how shall we console ourselves of our humble lot, we hapless cicadas of Parnassus?"[107] Considered the leading librettist and poet of his day, Metastasio's words are praise indeed.

In 1750, Maria Antonia sent a copy of *Trionfo* to Metastasio, for critique and perhaps seeking his advice on its style. According to Weber, Metastasio edited the work too thoroughly, so much so that Maria Antonia wrote to Prime Minister Brühl that "Metastasio has cruelly mutilated it, he left not one of my airs alone which brings me to tears and what's more, is that he has changed them so that not one of my airs would fit them."[108] The rest of the correspondence between the Princess Royal and the Prime Minister in the summer of 1750 shows that the pastoral in its original version was well received by all at court, especially by the King and Queen. They were in agreement with Maria Antonia that the revisions Metastasio made to the libretto upset

---

106 "Io non avrei mai in eterno saputo imaginarmi che una principessa giungesse a scrivere in poesia, ed in una lingua straniera, con questa eccellenza. Nelle due cantate e nella canzonetta non è solo ammirabile l'aggiustatezza delicata de' pensieri, la connessione delle idee, la nobilità della frase, l'armonia del verso e la scelta tenerezza dell'espressione; ma quello che più mi sorprende è una certa artificiosa facilità, per la quale non bastano i felici naturali talenti, ma si suppone una fermezza di polso che non si acquista se non se con lungo ed assiduo esercizio. . ." Metastasio, *Tutte le Opere*, Vol 3, p. 368. (There are at least nine letters in his collection which make reference to Maria Antonia, only one or two of which appear to have been known to Weber.)

107 "Oh poveri noi, caro Pasquini! Se i soverani scrivono in poesia in tale eccellenza, come ci consoleremo dell'umile nostra sorte noi sventurate cicale di Parnaso?" *Tutte le Opere*, Vol 3, p. 371.

108 "Metastasio l'a cruellement mutilé, il n'en a pas laisser un seul de mes airs dont je voudrait pleurer et ce qu'il y a de pis, c'est qu'il l'a changer de facon, que quant on le voudrait, on ne pourait y metre mes airs." Original as quoted in von Weber, p. 65. The letter from 22 July 1750 appears to no longer exist.

the balance of the work. They requested Maria Antonia send them the original version of her work, which she did.[109]

Also in the summer of 1750, it appears that Maria Antonia planned to have Hasse oversee a performance of *Trionfo* in Versailles for Maria Josepha, Dauphine.[110] Maria Antonia would have preferred to have the original version of *Trionfo* performed, but Metastasio was taking too long in sending back the original. To this, Prime Minister Brühl counseled her to send the revised version of the pastoral to Hasse and that perhaps he could find time before leaving Versailles to set the work to music, especially the earliest arias in the work. The Prime Minister believed Hasse ". . . will be up in arms against Metastasio for having overturned the idea of your Pastorale"[111]

Here we lose sight of the first edition of *Trionfo*. Hasse's biographer[112] states that Hasse did not wish to set Maria Antonia's pastoral. Indeed, the premiere performance of Hasse's setting of Maria Antonia's *La conversione di Sant'Agostino* had just taken place in the chapel of Taschenbergpalais in March 1750. By summer, he and Faustina Bordoni were performing throughout Europe, and he did not have the time to set another large dramatic text.

Weber, Fürstenau, and Yorke-Long have deployed this series of letters as proof that Maria Antonia did not write *Trionfo*, or that, at best, she should have claimed only partial authorship, with the "real" authors being Metastasio and Hasse. However, there is no evidence that

---

109 These sentiments are in a letter from Maria Josepha dated 12 August 1750 in which she states, "Je vous remercie de l'originale du Pastorale. Le R. l'asenci scait quand je pourray lire l'un et l'autre mais je ne peux pas pardonera Metastasio de l'avoir bouleversé." [I thank you for the original of the Pastoral. The King is in agreement and when I could read the one and the other but I can not forgive Metastasio to have upset it.]

110 This Maria Josepha was the eldest daughter of Friedrich August II and Maria Josepha. She was especially interested in maintaining cultural ties with the Dresden court, whether it was through importation of Meissen porcelain or the importation of musicians and artists from the Saxon court.

111 ". . . sera en courroux contre Metastasio d'avoir entierment boulverse l'idee de Votre Pastorale." Also quoted in von Weber, p. 68.

112 *New Grove*, 2000.

Hasse ever saw *Trionfo* in its revised or original state. There is no copy of *Trionfo* bearing editorial corrections. Furthermore, it is implausible that Maria Antonia, having set her opera to her satisfaction, would abandon it to the ministrations of another composer. Certainly, neither Metastasio nor Hasse claimed authorship of a work with the title *Il trionfo della fedeltà*. Consequently, 19th- and 20th-century authors have privileged male over female claims to authorship in such a way that the female authorial voice can only be heard as inauthentic. This further privileges paid, professional creativity over unpaid, amateur creativity.

Maria Antonia likely wrote *Trionfo*, set it to music, and performed it in a private family setting with a cast that included other family members and nobles. Then, after receiving encouragement from Pasquini and Metastasio, she sent it to the latter, and was displeased with his revisions. Only after expressing her displeasure was she persuaded by her spouse, Pasquini, and others to rewrite the music and text herself, which she did, taking Metastasio's "corrections" into account, but not adopting them wholesale. Thus in 1754, a new libretto was copied, and the work was again performed. This scenario is supported by evidence not noted by previous biographers: letters from Graf von Wackerbarth, Privy Councillor to Friedrich Christian. They describe the daily lives of the royal family, their friends, and courtiers, in Dresden to the Prime Minister, who must give a full account to the King and Queen in Warsaw.

These letters, written every two days or so, give insights into life at the court. Their days were filled with ceremonial duties and opportunities to enjoy music and theater performances. Sometimes they created the theatrical events themselves. A letter from 15 Novembre 1750 states: "M:ʳ the Chamberlain of S:ᵗ Sernin is preparing to give next Thursday with several Cavaliers and Ladies of the City the complete performance of the Tragedy <u>Zayre</u> to Madame the Royal Electoral

Princess in her apartments."[113] A letter dated 20 Novembre 1750 contains a cast list for that production. No fewer than four letters from Graf von Wackerbarth provide evidence in favor of Maria Antonia's sole production of *Trionfo*:[114]

> Dresden 3 April 1754
> .... After dining Madame the Electoral Princess regaled him [Friedrich Christian] with a preview of the beautiful Pastoral for which She composed, Herself, both the words and the music, and which is of admirable taste. . .

> Dresden 22 April 1754 The day before yesterday in the evening Madame the Princess Royal Electoral held a run through of her Pastoral. We have not yet heard the third Act. It must be still more beautiful than the two others. You can, Monseigneur judge from that the whole work.

> Dresden 19 June 1754
> .... The day before yesterday Their Royal Electoral Highnesses walked in Your Excellence's garden, with the two Priests, but They were taken by surprise by a violent storm which obliged them to return to Town, where later They passed the evening at a gaming party in the apartments of Madame the Princess. Yesterday the last rehearsal of the Pastoral took place to which Their Royal Electoral Highnesses wanted to admit several Cavaliers and Ladies of the City. It only lacked the incomparable Director of pleasures of Their Royal Electoral Highnesses whose presence would have given still more relief to this beautiful music. . .

---

113 "M.ʳ le Chambellan de S.ᵗ Sernin se prépare à donner Jeudi prochain avec plusieurs Cavaliers et Dames de la Ville l'epreuve generale de la Tragedie Zayre à Madame la Princesse Roïale Electorale dans ses appartemens."

114 Loc. 3058, Vol IV 1753 & 1754.

Dresden 28 August 1754

. . . . Yesterday afternoon Madame the Princess Electoral rehearsed again her beautiful Pastoral. The two bavarian Chamberlains Mr le Comte de Minuzzi and Mr le Baron de Klingenberg were also admitted to it. At the end of the first act Mr le Chevalier Williams, who had only just arrived in Dresden, came forward to render his respects to Their Royal Highnesses who gave to him the most gracious (respects] in the world. . .[115]

From these performances alone, Maria Antonia became known in her own court and throughout Europe as the composer and librettist to this opera. The libretto was printed by the court publisher Walther in this same year. In a city where 99% of the businesses had direct

---

115 "à Dresde ce 3 Avril 1754
. . . . Après diner Madame la Princesse Electorale le [Friedrich Christian] régala d'une épreuve de la belle Pastorale dont Elle a composé Elle même les vers et la Musique, et qui est d'un gout tout admirable. . .

à Dresde ce 22 Avril 1754
Avant hier au soir Madame la Princesse Roiale Elect^le fit faire un essai general de sa Pastorale. L'on n'en avoit pas encor entendû le troisieme Acte. Il fût trouve encor plus beau que les deux autres. Vous pourrés, Monseigneur juger par là de toute la piece. . .

à Dresde ce 19 Juin 1754
. . . . Avant hier L. A. R.^Elles furent au jardin de Votre Excellence, avec les deux Nonces, mais Elles y furent surprise d'un violent orage qui les obligea de s'en retourner en Ville, où ensuite Elles passerent la soirée à une partie de jeu dans les appartemens de Mad^e la Princesse. Hier il y eut la derniere répetition de la Pastorale à la quelle L. A. R. E.^les ont bien voulû admetre plusieurs Cavaliers et Dames de la Ville. Il n'y manquer que l'incomparable Directeur des plaisirs de L. A. R. E.^les dans la presence auroit donné encor plus de rélief à cette belle musique. . . .

à Dresde ce 28 Aout 1754
. . . . Hier après midi Madame la Princesse Electoral fit de nouveau la repetition de sa belle Pastorale. Les deux Chambellans Bavarois Mr le Comte de Minuzzi et Mr le Baron de Klingenberg ý furent aussi admis. Sur la fin du premier acte Mr. Le Chevalier de Williams, qui ne fasoit qu'arriver à Dresde, vint sur le champ rendre ses respects à LL AA RR qui le recûrent les plus gracieusement du monde. . ."

The letters to and from Wackerbarth merely scratch the surface. The Comtesse de Lodron was one of Maria Antonia's attendants, and sent reports about the Princess' health to the Queen. A study of life at the courts of Dresden and Poland using these sources has yet to be undertaken.

or indirect connections to the court,[116] Walther had been the printer to the royal family for generations. Eventually, nearly all of Maria Antonia's works would be published by Dresden or Leipzig publishers. In this way, Maria Antonia made certain that her creative works could also be seen as acts of patronage. Her creativity was not only a personal endeavor, but one that would have benefits for Saxony's citizens.

There is no evidence of a version of Maria Antonia's *Trionfo* that was set by Hasse, nor are any letters between these two composers known to exist.[117] A manuscript entitled *Il trionfo della fedeltà* surfaced in Berlin at the court of Frederick II in the year 1753. Although it is presently cataloged under Hasse's name, it comprises the work of other authors, in addition to Hasse: Frederick II and the professional composers Georg Benda and Carl Heinrich Graun. It is less an opera than a grouping of arias, most without recitatives. The texts take a mocking attitude towards the themes of love and fidelity, which is likely a reflection of Frederick's own attitude toward the subject.

Consider, for example, this aria by Frederick himself: "Pensa ch'io son fedele, pensa ch'è il mio tesoro, ch'io l'amo, ch'io l'adoro."[118] None of the texts in this manuscript bears any relation to Maria Antonia's *Trionfo*, or to her view of fidelity as a sacrament. Perhaps she heard about this production and ensured that her libretto was printed in order to establish herself as its author. There might be another reason, however, and that has to do with the influence of one of the most well-known couples of the middle-18th century: Johann and Luise Gottsched.

The Gottscheds sought to unify and elevate German literary culture through their publications and through teaching. They, particularly

---

116 Stadtarchiv Dresden und seine Bestände, p. 151.

117 It is possible that research in the royal archives at the Bibliotheque Nationale, Paris, would clarify the musical events of the summer of 1750.

118 15 "She thinks that I am faithful, thinks that she is my treasure, that I love her, that I adore her."

Johann Christoph Gottsched, were seen in the 18th century as leading this movement. Luise Adelgunde Kalmus, later Gottsched, was born in Danzig (now Gdansk, Poland). Her parents gave her an education that included music and languages. After a long correspondence, she married Johann Christoph Gottsched and came with him to Leipzig.

She was his research assistant, editor, and secretary, but she also continued to improve her command of foreign languages through translations of foreign dramas. In 1750, Luise Gottsched published a translation of the history of the French Royal Academy of Sciences. Although she spent a good deal of her life editing her spouse's writings, Luise Gottsched was known and respected as a playwright, journalist, and translator.

Maria Antonia and Friedrich Christian made regular visits to the university town of Leipzig, often attending lectures by Johann Christoph Gottsched. Luise Gottsched apparently first learned of Maria Antonia's literary activities through Graf von Manteuffel, as can be seen in letters between Manteuffel and Wackerbarth. In 1748, Maria Antonia wrote a paraphrase of the *Miserere* which would later be published under the pseudonym "Madame D***" as *Sentimens d'une Ame Pénitente Sur le Pseaume Miserere*. So full of praise was Manteuffel that he sought to learn its author.

He discovered in a letter dated 16 July 1748 the initials "M. A. R. P. E." [for Maria Antonia Royale Princesse Electorale], "which have served to assure me of the rightness of my guess."[119] He spread word of this work through his circle of friends which included the Gottscheds.

---

119 "qui ont achevé de m'assûrer de la justesse de ma divination." There is possibly a connection between Graf von Manteuffel and the publisher Walther, as this exerpt from another letter shows: 28 June 1748 Monseigneur .... Votre Excellence aiant eu la beauté de m'envoyer une magnifique paraphrase du Ps. Miserere, j'ai chargé Mr. De Walther de Lui presenter une Meditation, ou paraphrase pareille du Ps 15 en prose..."

Luise Gottsched was as taken with the work as was Manteuffel, and wanted to meet the author.[120]

The date of Maria Antonia and Luise Gottsched's first meeting is not certain. Certainly by 1754 they were aware enough of each other's interests because it was during that theater season that the Gottscheds presented the Princess Royal with their translation of her first opera. It was also in this year that Johann Gottsched published his *Einladungschrift, von der Arkadischen Gesellschaft zu Rom*,[121] an appeal to other members of the Leipzig Academy of Fine Arts (founded by Johann Christoph Gottsched and others) to establish a literary society based on the model of Rome's Arcadian Academy. It is highly likely that this idea grew out of discussions with the princely couple, whose own Arcadian membership was widely known. It names both Maria Antonia and Friedrich Christian and provides strong evidence of

---

120 Letter dated 8 Aout 1748,
"Monseigneur
Ne pouvant douter, que ma derniere letter; qui étoit du 26 d. p. ; new soit arrivée à bon part, Votre Excellence ne sauroit trouver extraordinaire, que je commence la presente, comme je finissois celle-là; c. A d. Par Vous entretenir de cette Divine Paraphrase du Miserere, qui est le sujet du mone, dont la reception m'a le plus penetré de plaisir, et d'admiration.
Mon amour propre aiant été agréablement flatté, par l'ordre gracieux, que l'auteur, lui-meme, Vous avoit donné, Monseigneur, de m'envoier cette Divine Piece, je n'ai pu m'empecher de la communiquer à mes amis. Et comme il y en a un, parmi eux, qui publie, tous les mois, un journal litteraire, il est arrivé, qu' aiant été tant entousiasmé de cet admirable poéme, il en a donné un extrait dans sa brochure periodique, dont je prens la liberté de joindre ici deux exemplaire.
Cet extrait, assez savamment énoncé, ce me semble; a quelque chose de singuliier. C'est qu'il est fait par une femme savant. . ."
11 Aout 1748
". . . Votre Excellence voulait d'ailleurs, que je Lui dise, si l'on ne s'est point trompé, en devinant l'auteur de l'extrait dont il est question, je puis Vous assurer, Monseigneur, qu'on a rencontré, il ne se peut pas mieux. C'est Mad. Gottsched, qui l'a fait, et elle est toute glorieuse de l'approbation de Mad. la Pr. Roïale, et de l'esperance de se voir gratifiée de l'exemplaire, qu'elle ambitionne."
20 Aout 1748
". . . J'ai l'honneur d'accuser la reception de Vos lignes du 16 d. c., et, en même tems, celle du nouvel exemplaire de l'admirable paraphrase du Miserere. Je n'ai pas manqué de la faire tenir incessamment, suivant ceux du modéle des Muses; à Mad. G. , qui est toute transportée de joie et de reconnoissance. . ."
121 *Sammlung einiger Ausgesuchten Stücke. der Gesellschaft der freyen Künste zu Leipzig. Theil 1*. p. 165.

mutual interest in the creation of a German literary culture based on Italian models.[122]

Johann Christoph Gottsched translated the libretto to *Trionfo* into German and presented it to the Princess in mid-1754. He had earlier translated her oratorio *La conversione*. Later, a translation of *Talestri* would follow. The Gottscheds visited Dresden and attended a production by Johann Leppert's comedy troupe[123] of Luise Gottsched's *Die ungleiche Heyrath* (*The Unequal Marriage*). The production of this play was a gift from Maria Antonia and Friedrich Christian to the Gottscheds for the translation.[124] In light of Suzanne Kord's research, it may be that Luise Gottsched had more than a little to do with the translation of Maria Antonia's works.

The German Enlightenment has traditionally been viewed as owing to English or French models without having its own character. However, it is clear from the work of Maria Antonia and the Gottscheds that German enlightenment authors were searching for a way to break with French literary models. The creation of a secular German culture that took a broader, more European view was the work of the 18th century, not, as is often presumed, the 19th century.

The language of the nobility remained French, and the language of those at university was, additionally, Latin. However, the musical culture, which was a mixture of French and Italian influences, and the trend toward Italian music and literature had increased during the reign of Friedrich August II/August III. In the 1750s, authors like the Gottscheds began to see these Italian texts as a framework thorough which they could create a native German literary tradition.

---

122 The volume notably is dedicated, not to the King, but to Prince Friedrich Christian.
123 Johann Martin Leppert was the director of the Hofkomödianten (court comedians).
124 *Das geheime politische Tagebuch des Kurprinzen Friedrich 1751 bis 1757*, p. 228-9.

German Reform of the Arts

In the Enlightenment, many within the German princely states were throwing off the courtly ideals of France in an attempt to create a more authentically German culture. They did not merely look inward, but rather turned their eyes southward to the land seen as the font of classical culture: Italy. From the creation of academies to the performance of music, Maria Antonia and the circle around her may seem to have used Italian models as a way of learning to create a German national culture. This national culture does not have the unification of these German states as its goal. This 18th-century nationalism is distinctly local in flavor. It promotes "Saxon patriots," to paraphrase Johann Gottsched, and therefore expects its aristocracy to appoint and train its own citizens in the classical arts rather than hire court musicians and artists from other lands. This nationalism promotes the German language as the equal of French or Italian, and therefore, as perfectly appropriate for serious poetry and drama.

The movement to reform German theater and to uplift German literary language was one of which the Gottscheds were an integral part. Lacking indigenous examples of refined literature, writers had long turned to French sources in translation for the stage. The translation of Italian works into German would offer respite from the influence of Francophile culture. Especially heartening to the Gottscheds must have been the fact that this Italian work had been written by the future Electress of Saxony. That Maria Antonia agreed to have her work translated into German shows that she was at the forefront of creating a culture of refinement in Saxony that could hold its own with the art and culture of the other courts in Europe. This parallels her support of the painter Anton Raphael Mengs and patronage of native composers such as Schürer and Naumann.

Just as a unique Saxon identity in the arts was beginning to gestate, its development would unfortunately be put to a halt. By 1756, war would rear its ugly head and become an obstacle to any plans for artistic reform.

Chapter 9
The Seven Years' War and Beyond

The War Years, 1756-1763

During the Seven Years' War, Saxony was ransacked, bombarded, and virtually bankrupted in the war that would expand the King of Prussia's sphere of influence at Saxony and Austria's expense. Maria Antonia was responsible in large measure for keeping the spirit of the royal family up during the occupation of Dresden by Frederick II of Prussia.

The family was split. The King fled for strategic reasons to his court in Warsaw, bringing with him some of the court musicians. Maria Josepha remained in Dresden to be an example for and protectress to the Catholics of that city. Maria Antonia's eldest sons—Friedrich August, Anton, and Maximilian—were sent to Prague for their safety. Princes Xaver and Albert, Friedrich Christian's brothers, were actively engaged in leading troops into battle. The rest of the princes and princesses remained at court. The musical establishment of the Residenzschloss was greatly reduced, although Mass continued to be performed in the Catholic church. An indication of the state of siege that Saxony found itself in is that the *Hof-Calender*, the yearly publication of the goings-on at court, ceased publication.

A politically motivated gesture of friendship from Maria Antonia to Frederick II was her gift to him of a copy of *Trionfo*. This won her his admiration and respect, for they shared a passionate interest in the arts. Perhaps it was hoped that an artistic admiration could ease the harshness of the Prussian King's political and military policy. She would eventually tire of the gentle condescension in his refusal to deal with her as a political equal, but Maria Antonia and Frederick remained correspondents for the next twenty years.

In 1757, Maria Josepha died following a stroke. Books and poems were published celebrating her as a good and pious Catholic. This turn of events darkened the mood at court, and left Maria Antonia in complete control of the musical life at court. Now the princely apartments would be the center of musical life at Dresden. Now the Princess Royal had laudatory cantatas sung to her. The *Componimento per musica da cantarsi il di 13 Giungno 1758 per festiggiare il nome di Ermelinda Talea P. A.*, for example, was performed for her by the Princesses Elisabeth and Cunigunde.

Also during this time of greatly reduced forces, local composers such as Johann Schürer became more important in the musical life at court. He had composed music for cantatas dedicated to various members of the royal family at least since the late 1740s. Now he was given the task of composing a yearly mass for Maria Antonia's patron saint, Saint Anthony of Padua, which he did for each year from 1758 through 1764, except for 1759.

In 1759, the Saxon royal family fled for safety from Dresden to Munich. A portrait dating from 1761 and on display in Munich's Schloss Nymphenburg shows the combined Saxon and Bavarian electoral and royal families during the Saxon family's exile and allows a further glimpse into their private lives. From it one gets a sense of what some of those musical evenings were like: some members of the family are playing cards, others are making music (Prince Carl of Saxony on flute; Margravine von Baden Maria Josepha [Maria Antonia's sister] at the harpsichord; Clemens August, Elector of Cologne [Maria Antonia's uncle] on violoncello; and Princess Elisabeth of Saxony singing), others are drinking coffee, including Maria Antonia. A lute leans on the wall near Maria Antonia, the only hint that she, too, is a musician. Only two of Maria Antonia and Friedrich Christian's children are portrayed: Princess Maria Amalia and Prince Carl. In contrast to many other portraits, this was clearly meant to be a private painting, for the eyes of family and friends alone. It is the only portrait that shows Friedrich Christian not in a heroic standing pose, but in a wheelchair being pushed by Graf Wackerbarth.

Both Friedrich Christian and Maria Antonia would witness the signing of the Treaty of the Peace of Hubertusburg in 1763. Peace with the Prussians meant the King's return to Dresden, and the joint handling of political developments by the Prince and Princess Royal was seemingly forgotten. Friedrich August II was intent on showing the court in its pre-war splendor. Maria Antonia was asked to sing in royal command performances of her second opera, *Talestri, regina delle amazzoni* and of an opera by Hasse. A change in Maria Antonia's attitudes toward performance can be seen in the September 1763 letter she sent her cousin, the

Empress Maria Theresia:

I am quite obliged to Count Sternberg, who made a very beautiful painting for my opera. If I could have the happiness to sing it in front of Your Majesty, the envy of pleasing you would be the best form of success. However, I must tell you in confidence that this opera has given me a great deal of pain. I only let myself be engaged to sing it in order to give our king testimony of our joy for his happy return, and unfortunately it has given birth to the desire to have us perform it in front of others; at present, Leucippo is on tap, that Leucippo that has already been sung by everyone! I do what I can, to dispense with it, but I am told that the king wants it, what can I do? *This has caused me true aggravation; after having been during the last few years engaged in some very serious and quite useful occupations, it is really sad to see oneself reduced to the job of a singer! It no longer fits my age, nor my station; what will the public think, which has begun to take a good opinion of me? It will say that I only love frivolous talents, and will perhaps dispute the little merit I have acquired.* Ah, my dear friend, pardon, if I open my heart to you on a chapter which I should more sensibly only dare to confide in a person of a certain age![125] (italics mine).

That Maria Antonia should view the profession of singing so negatively is in keeping with what is known of 18th-century attitudes towards women as performers. It was perfectly fine for a woman to

---

125 "J'ay bien de l'obligation au conte de Sternberg, de ce qu'il a fait un tableau si favorable de mon opera; si j'avois pu avoir le bonheur de le chanter devant Votre Majesté, l'envie de luy plaire d'auroit fait d'autant mieu reussir. Cependant je dois luy dire confidement que cet opera a eu des suittes qui me fond de la peine. Je ne me suis laissés engager a le chanter que pour doner a notre roy un temoignage de notre joje [joie] pour son heureu retour, et malheuesement il a tant plus qu'il a fait naitre l'envie de nous en faire jouer encore d'autres; a present Leucippo est sur le tapis, ce Leucippo que tout le monde a deja chantéz! Je fait ce que je puis, pour m'en dispencer, mais on me dit que le roy le desire, que pui-je faire? *Cela me cause un vray chagrin: après avoir étés pendant tant d'année livrée a des occupationes plus serieuses et plus uttilles, il est bien triste de se voir reduite au metier de chanteuse! Cela ne convient plus ny a mon age, ny a mon etat; que pencera le public qui avoit comencé a prendre bone opinion de moy? Il dira que je n'aime que les tallents frivoles, et me disputera peut-etre le peu de merite que j'ay aquis.* Ah, ma chere amie, pardoné, si je vous ay ouvert mon coeur sur un chapitre qui m'est d'autant plus senssible que je n'ose confier mon chagrin a persone depuy une certaine epoque!" Letter in Lippert, p. 175-176. Italics mine.

perform in private, but women on the stage were held in very low esteem. This was still a time when actors and playwrights could not be buried in cemeteries and were chased out of their residences as they lay on their deathbeds so that their landlords would not have the taint of their deaths on their consciences.[126]

Of course, since letter writing between royals was never a purely private affair, perhaps this letter has a very public political purpose. In it, Maria Antonia is not expressing an aversion to performance per se—since she would continue until the end of her life to perform privately—but rather a wish to distance herself from a public role that would not suit her increased status as the next Electress and Queen. After all, though portraits exist of the imperial children performing as dancers, none exist of the same people as adults in performance. The era of Louis XIV or August the Strong had long passed, and more was expected from their public person. No ruler, particularly a female one, could risk seeming "frivolous" if she wanted to maintain power. Of this, Maria Antonia was too aware.

The performances in the Kurprinzliches Reithaus auf dem Taschenberg in August and September of 1763 met with great success. They were publicized in the public newspapers and lauded inside court.[127] Then in October of that year, the King died following a stroke. Friedrich Christian became Elector, and Maria Antonia, Electress. At last, they would have the opportunity to implement their economic and cultural policies, but then in December, Maria Antonia's beloved spouse was taken from her. The sources disagree as to whether his death followed a stroke or some other malady, but in any case, Maria Antonia's reign came to an abrupt end.

---

126 I refer to the death of Catherine Neuber, the famous Leipzig playwright who was chased out of her residence during the last few days of her life.

127 See Dreßdnischer Merkwürdigkeiten, September 1763.

The Return to a Private Self, 1763-1780

Also to end was Maria Antonia's compositional life. Although much of the collected poetry by her cannot be dated with certainty, no new music emanated from her pen after *Talestri*. Perhaps the main reason that Maria Antonia ceased composing was the death of those for whom she enjoyed performing. Out of love and a desire to honor those closest to her, she created cantata texts for the King and Queen. She wrote her first opera first as a way of honoring the King, and her revised version was dedicated to her devoted spouse as one can surmise from the illustrations for the Stössel & Krause libretto of *Trionfo* that clearly show the monogram "FC" in an imaginary proscenium arch (Illustrations 9.1a & b).

With these key people gone, her creativity needed another outlet. She turned to activities that would be societally acceptable for a woman of her station: her painting and patronage of other artists. From 1764 onward, Maria Antonia's operas would be performed to her honor or to honor another beloved family member, but she would not write another note nor another word of poetry. She instead worked with her brother-in-law Xaver to implement her and Friedrich Christian's policies. Even though Xaver was appointed Administrator of Saxony and was the most public face of the royal family, he honored his late brother's wishes and made certain that Maria Antonia was always a witness to cabinet meetings, and therefore still a public figure. The Academy of Fine Arts she and Friedrich Christian had planned was established in March of 1764, with Maria Antonia, Prince Xaver, and Friedrich August IV in attendance. The next large-scale production of Maria Antonia's opera *Trionfo* was in 1767. It was performed for Prince

Xaver's name day, the 3rd of December.[128] Maria Antonia was now no longer the lead singer but one of the honored audience members.

She had control over the education of her children, supervising especially the musical education given to them by Peter August, her music secretary and chamber composer.[129] Once her son reached majority and married in 1769, Maria Antonia, as was to be expected, stepped out of the limelight. Her widow's pension was not large—no one had expected Friedrich Christian to die at such a young age.

His will stipulated that her place of residence must remain Dresden, but this did not forbid her from spending substantial portions of her remaining years elsewhere. At least half the year, Maria Antonia would live at her brother Maximilian III Joseph's court in Munich. She also traveled around Europe, perhaps in fulfillment of childhood dreams. Maria Antonia's trips were always accompanied by music-making. As her music had been composed to honor others, now it was performed to honor her.

Her long-delayed Grand Tour of Italy took place in 1772. In Padua, *Trionfo* was performed in the Teatro Nuovo during its off season specifically for her, which was doubtlessly arranged by fellow Arcadians. That same year, her cantata and opera texts were published in Rome, again by fellow Arcadians, as *Varj componimenti per musica di E. T. P. A.*

Back in German lands, Maria Antonia could be found leading the lists in a shooting contest held at Nymphenburg in 1775.[130] Though she may appear to 20th-century eyes to have vanished from public life following the death of her spouse, Maria Antonia was very much an important figure—and not just in Saxon politics. In 1777, following the death of her brother, she tried to win the succession for the Electoral

---

128 Oberhofmarschallamt, G73.

129 Friedrich August IV was quite well known and respected as a keyboardist, although he would not play in public.

130 Maria Antonia had distinguished herself earlier in this arena. She is the only Saxon Princess for which hunting weapons were made.

crown of Bavaria for her son. This failed due to her son's refusal of the crown. Hers was far from being a life lived in "growing isolation" as the *New Grove* puts it.[131] Maria Antonia lived her remaining years in Dresden and died there in April 1780. Her oratorio *La conversione di Sant'Agostino* was performed in the Basilica of St. Anthony of Padua in her honor.

Her Highness' Lasting Legacy

As the matriarch and musical guide of her family, Maria Antonia was crucial in the Wettins' renewed support of the arts after the Seven Years' War. Of her seven children, six survived into adulthood: Friedrich August, Karl, Anton, Maximilian, Maria Amalia, and Maria Anna. It is obvious from the fifty volumes of music left behind by Anton and the collection of music accumulated by Friedrich August that her love of Italian music and literature influenced theirs. Her granddaughter Maria Amalia (Maximilian's daughter) was undoubtedly inspired by her illustrious grandmother's example when she set about composing operas.

Friedrich August kept his mother informed of Dresden performances by exceptional musicians, especially those of the Italian violinist Maddalena Sirmen, whom the Electress had commended to the Berlin court many years previous.[132] The support of the Dresden court of home-grown musicians and composers, even though they were expected to compose in the Italian manner, was a direct outgrowth of Maria Antonia's style and interests.

Composers such as Naumann were trained and appointed with her backing. This certainly had ramifications for the musical life of Dresden. The court's support for the construction of the Semper Opera House, a

---

131 *New Grove*, "Maria Antonia Walpurgis."
132 In D: Dla, Nachlasse 1 Nr. 62. Briefe von und an Männer.

public opera house to replace earlier ones destroyed by warfare, would not have been possible without a royal family committed to the arts.

Maria Antonia considered herself a "Liebhaber"—a "dilettante" or amateur of the arts. If we are to understand her and the music and culture of the early modern period, we must remove from that word its negative connotations. She and other nobles like her, women especially, built community through the arts—especially music and poetry. This is perhaps the greatest contribution that non-professional musicians make; they create an environment where art and creativity can flourish through their patronage and in their own interest and active participation in creative activities.

Astutely regarding the expectations for women of her station, Maria Antonia made certain that her creativity was ultimately seen as a form of patronage, for the instrumentalists who accompanied her vocal works, for the singers who began their careers singing in her operas, for the publisher of her operas, and for the publishers of her poetry and prose works. Men and women actively sought her aid, whether Giovanni Ferrandini or Maria Teresa Agnesi or Maddalena Sirmen, or the countless others whose letters still exist in Maria Antonia's files in the Hauptstaatsarchiv in Dresden. In this way, she was able to conform to the 18th-century expectation of a good woman and wife while simultaneously expressing her creative soul.

Closing Words

I hope you enjoyed reading about Her Highness as much as I enjoyed researching her. Although much of this manuscript is twenty years old, I was pleasantly surprised that it needed only minor tweaks in order to be readied for publication, and that I agreed with nearly everything I had written way back when.

At this point, I wish I could offer you a CD or MP3 recording of the works I examined in this book. Alas, I cannot offer such a thing. When Virginia Woolf wrote in 1929 that it takes money and "a room of one's own" in order for a woman to write, she was right. Financial freedom and creative freedom go hand in hand. What Maria Antonia's life shows is that, more than just a room, one needs a palace and theater of one's own as well as an active, engaged creative community in order to experience success in the arts and in life.

If you feel that this book deserves to be an audiobook, complete with musical excerpts, please let me know. More importantly, let others know. Do you know a harpsichordist, violinist, or other 18th-century music aficionado I just have to meet? Feel free to introduce us! Perhaps you know of a venue that has a lecture series or are friends with a podcaster. Feel free to share this book with them! You, dear reader, are part of my active, engaged community, and with your support, my long-standing desire to record Maria Antonia's music can be realized.

Operas from this period are still rarely performed, and if they are, such productions are often done with a sense of modern irony and a complete misunderstanding of the composer's and librettist's intentions. For example, a recent production of Francesca Caccini's 1625 opera, *La liberazione di Ruggiero dall'isola d'Alcina* (*The Liberation of Ruggiero from Alcina's Island*) made life with the villain, Alcina, look more inviting than a life spent with the heroine (and "knight in shining armor") Bradamante. Operas in which virtues such as justice, prudence, temperance, faith, and love are rewarded are typical of the pre-19th-century stage, but I feel that our age does not fully appreciate such works. This is also likely the reason that Maria Antonia's second opera gets more airplay than her first. Its title, *Talestri, Regina delle amazzoni* (*Talestri, Queen of the Amazons*) seems to promise a work much more in line with popular mores than a work about fidelity. This is not entirely the case, but that is a discussion for another day.

Giving voice to Her Highness has helped me find my own voice. Ultimately, though, as enjoyable as it is to write another person's story, I find it even more satisfying to share my own. Therefore, the next project from the studio of April plus Madison is likely to be the publication *The Big Book of Madisonnets*. Wonderland draws me in the way Arcadia drew Maria Antonia in, and looking at the world through a Lewis Carroll–inspired lens has definitely enriched my postdoc life in ways I never could have imagined prior to 2010. Also in the works are talks and a course entitled, *Finding Your Voice*. Whether you sing, speak, or write—or want to—we all have challenges to overcome when it comes to freeing our voice and sharing it with others. I share strategies and techniques that can transform your relationship to your voice, your creativity and your life. Looking forward to seeing you off the page!

Appendix 1: Illustrations

Appendix 1: Illustrations

Chapter Two:

Illustration 2.1: Cover page to *Catalogo de[i] Libri.*

Illustration 2.2: Three different scribal hands

Illustration 2.3: Sample page with "Munich 8"

Chapter Four:

Illustration 4.1: Maria Antonia's aria book, opening page

Illustration 4.2: Opening page to "Meditationes"

Illustration 4.3: *Perfido mi tradisti* excerpts

Illustration 4.4: *Barbaro dispietato* excerpts

Illustration 4.5: *Quanto è felice* excerpts

Illustration 4.6: *Prendi l'ultimo addio* excerpts

Illustration 4.7: *Grande Augusto* excerpts

Appendix 2: Primary Sources

My list supplements that which was found in Drewes and Petzholdt in that an attempt has been made to list works that are currently extant. For a listing of Maria Antonia's paintings, see von Weber. This is the first time that English-language descriptions of most of these materials are appearing in print.

I have used these RISM sigla for the different libraries:

D: Dla is the Hauptstaatsarchiv, Dresden

D: Dlb is the Sächsische Landesbibliothek

US: Cah is Cambridge, Mass., Houghton Library, Harvard University

US: NYp is New York, N. Y., New York Public Library at Lincoln Center

Further abbreviations:

KÖB = Königliche Öffentliche Bibliothek

KPMS = Königliche Privatmusik Sammlung

SLB = Sächsische Landesbibliothek

kbd = keyboard

hpsch. = harpsichord

Ms. = manuscript

The list, while thorough, is not meant to be exhaustive. I have restricted it mainly to Dresden sources, however in some cases, the first and best source consulted is elsewhere.

Part 1: Music and Texts by Maria Antonia
Scores

Arie sei composte da N. (Ms Score, c. 1747).

Dlb (Mus 3119-F-11 + 11a)

Dlb (Mus 3119-F-10)

Variazione e cadenze dell'Aria a Oboe Solo (Ms. Score, c. 1754).

Dlb (Mus 3119-F-5b)

"Al tempio al tempio andiamo." (Ms. score. Voice/kbd, c. 1754).

Dlb (Mus. 3119-F-8)

Il trionfo della fedeltà. Dramma pastorale per musica di E. T. P. A. (Leipzig: Johann Gottlob Immanuel Breitkopf, 1756).

Dlb (Mus. 3119-F-5-& 5a, with parts)

Overture from *Il trionfo della fedeltà.* In: *Raccolta delle megliore sinfonie di piu celebri compositori di nostro tempo, accomodate all clavicembalo.* (Leipzig: G. G. I. Breitkopf, 1761 [-62]), Vol 2, pp 1-6. hpsch. Print.

Dlb (Mus. 1-N-7)

Talestri, regina delle amazzoni. Dramma per musica di E. T. P. A.
(Leipzig: Breitkopf, 1765). Dlb (Mus 3119-f-500)

    Dlb (Mus 3119-F-2 & 2a) (Ms Score)

Libretti

Die Bekehrung des heil. Augustini. (Ms copy, c. 1750).

*Il Trionfo/ Della Fedeltà./ Favola Pastorale,/ per Musical Da rappre-
sentarsi nel Reale Teatro di/*[empty space]/ *In occasione del felicissimo
giorno Natalizio/ Di S. M. Il Re di Pollonia &c./*[KÖB stamp]/ [SLB
stamp] (Ms, c. 1748).

    Dlb (Rara MT.4.114) Ms, c. 1748

    Dlb (Rara MT. 4.115) Ms, c. 1748

Il Trionfo/ della/ Fedeltà./ [KPMS stamp]/ [KÖB stamp]/ [SLB
stamp] (Ms, c. 1754).

    Dlb (MT.4.113 Rara) Ms, c. 1754

Il trionfo della fedeltà. Dramma pastorale per musica di E. T. P. A.
(Dresden: Stössel & Krause, 1754).

    US: NYp

Der / Sieg der Treue./ [ornate line] / *Ein gesungenes Schäferspiel/ von/
E. T.P.A./* (flower) / [lines] / *DRESDEN, / Gedruckt in der Churfürstli.
Hofbuchdruckerey./* 1767.

    Dlb (MT 1283)

Il trionfo della fedeltà. (Vienna, Nella stampiera di Ghelen, 1768).

US: CAh

TALESTRI / Regina / delle Amazzoni / Dramma per musica / Di / E. T. P. A. / Dresda/ Per la Regia Stamperia / MDCCLXIII. [1763].

Dlb (MT 1282)

Thalestris / Königinn der Amazonen / [double line] / *aus dem/ vortrefflichen italienischen/ Singespiele/ Ihrer K*öniglichen Hoheit/ der unvergleichlichen /. Ermelinde Thalea / [lines] / *in ein / Deutsches Trauerspiel / verwandelt / von / Johann Christoph Gottscheden.* / [line] / *Zwickau, zu finden bey Christian Lebrecht Stielern.* [MA surmounted by a crown stamp] [SLB stamp]

Dlb MT.4.171 Rara:

TALESTRI,/ REGINA/ DELLE/ AMMAZONI, OPERA DRAMMATICA/ di/ E. T. P. A. / [printer's mark] / [lines] / *Dresda,* MDCCLXX. (1770) / STAMPATA DA C.S. WALTHER, / Librajo-Stampatore della Corte. [all within an 18th c border] [stamp of Stadtbibliothek Dresden at top of page, SLB stamp on bottom of page]

Dlb MT 1281

Libretti by Maria Antonia, Music by others

Music by Hasse

I. *La conversione di Sant'Agostino*

Dlb (Mus 2477-D-21)

Dlb (Mus 2477-D-22)

Dlb (Mus 2477-D-500)

Libretto

    Dlb (MT 4. 112 Rara)

II. Cantatas: *Grande Augusto* & *Che ti dirò, Regina*

    Dlb (Mus 2477-J-2)

    Dlb (Mus 2477-J-3,1 & 2)

    Dlb (Mus 2477-5-4 & 4a)

Music by Ristori

Didone abbandonata (1748)

    Dlb (Mus 2455-1-2 & 2a)

Lavinia a Turno (1748)

    Dlb (Mus 2455-1-1)

Nice e Tirsi (1749)

    Dlb (Mus 2455-1-3)

Music by Ferrandini

Cantata (text by Maria Antonia?)

    Dlb (Mus 3037-1-1)

Talestri

    Dlb (Mus 3037-F-4 & 4a)

Music by Naumann

Didone abbandonata

    Dlb (Mus 3480-1-6)

Lavinia a Turno

Dlb (Mus 3480-1-5,4)

Music by Manna (Text by Maria Antonia?)

Addio di Nice à Tirsi

Dlb (Mus 3105-L-1 & 1a)

Collections of Poetry and other publications by Maria Antonia

Sentimens d'une Ame Pénitente Sur le Pseaume Miserere Par Madame D*** traduits en vers. (Munich, 1747).

Dlb (32.4.538)

Poesies d' E. T. [P. A]. [Ermelinda Talea Pastorella Arcada] (c. 1750)

Dlb: Handschriftenabteilung

Varj componimenti della musica di E. T. P. A. (Rome, 1772).

US: CAh

Collections of Poetry by Maria Antonia and other Arcadians

Raccolta di Varie Poesie [Collection of Italian poetry]. (Ms, c. 1750).

Dlb: Handschriftenabteilung

Works Wrongly Attributed to Maria Antonia

Meditationes. Lib. 1. 2. Mediationes Secondo lib. 1. 2. Prologus and Chorus. (Ms. Score, 1746). 4 vol.

Dlb (Mus. 3119-D-2)

Notes: Eitner gives the date as 1746, and goes on to say, "Einer unverbürgten Nachricht zufolge werden die 4 Bände Kompos. ihr zugeschrieben. (According to an unverified message, the 4 volumes of compos[itions]. are attributed to her)"

Having looked at these, and at the photocopy of the text that is included, I would say these are not Maria Antonia's work based, in part, on the lack of female characters within. I posit that she might have had them copied for her own personal use. The photocopy of the original 18th-century texts reads: MISERICORDIA /DEI/ ARGUMENTUM/ QUATUOR MEDITATIONUM/*QUAS*/Congregation Latina Major/ *MATRIS PROPITIÆ*/ B.V. MARIÆ ab Angelo salutatæ/ *Quadragesimæ Tempore*/INSTITUIT/ MONACHII ANNO MDCCXLVI. / MEDITATIO II./ MISERICORDIA PUNIENS/ *SIVE*/FILIUS PRODIGUS/ in Servitute./ [line] /Typis Joannis Jacobi Vötter.

Written on the bottom of the previous page, there is this: "NB. NB. Domenica *in Albis* hora 4ta vespertina cantabuntur Vigiliæ, & die Lunæ sequeate solemnes Exequiæ in Oratoria sien pro Augustissimo Imperatore CAROLO VII. Ad eas sua præsentia honorandas DD. Sodales humanissimè invitantur. It seems to be connected with a memorial service for her father.

There are PERSONÆ MUSICÆ (musicians)listed in Meditation I. They are: "In Prologo. *Fides.* Jos. Wolf, Synt. A. B. *Ratio.* Franc. Xav. Ertl, Synt. A. A. *In Choro. Providentia,* Joseph Obermiller, Hum. B. *Genius Juventuis,* Michaël Echtler, Synt. A. B. *Tutor,* Greg. Est, Hum. A."

Motetti spirituali per la chiesa. (Ms. Score. 1730)

    Dlb (Mus 3119-D-1)

Notes: Her name on the title page indicates ownership.

Pastorale. Ms. Score. (1741)

    Dlb (Mus 3119-D-1)

Notes: Eitner calls this attribution questionable, and I concur.

Intermezzi comiche

Notes: Because it says "Maria Anton: Dux Bavariae" on the title page, this was wrongly attributed to Maria Antonia until 1966. It is from c. 1740 and was copied in Munich. Previous researchers have determined that it is a Telemann work, and it is now shelved accordingly [D: Dlb Mus 2392-F-1].

30 Arias Ms. Score (c. 1740).

Notes: See chapter 4 of the present work for commentary.

Part 2: Works Dedicated to Maria Antonia

This section contains both musical and non-musical dedications to the Electress. It is arranged chronologically.

1747

CONCORDIA /PAX, ET AMOR,/INTER ARMATÆ EVROPÆ DISCORDIAS/ TERRIS RESTITVTA/ PER AVGVSTISSSIMVM HYMENÆVM/ INTER/ SERENISSIMOS/**MAXIMILIANVM,/** ELECTOREM BAVARIÆ, / **MARIAM,**/REGIAM POLON. ELECTORALEM SAXONIÆ PRINCIPEM/NEC NON INTER/SERENISSIMOS/**FRIDERICUM,/** REGIUM POLON. ELECTORALEM SAXONIAE,/ **ANTONIAM,/** IMPERATORIAM ET ELECTORALEM BAVARIÆ/ PRINCIPES./*DRESDÆ CELEBRATVM./* ANNO

1747. MENSE JVNIO./[LINE] /DRESDÆ, LITTERIS HARPETERIANIS. [KÖB STAMP]

Notes: Dlb call number: Hist Sax. C 1140

6' x 8"

Rose fabric covered. Vander Ley paper (hunting horn in scallopped shield) as cover sheet. Gilded pages. Printed source. Latin poetry dedicated to the marrying couples.

AD AVIENDAS/ ORATIONES BINAS PANEGYRICAS/ QVIBVS/ SERENISSIMO PRINCIPI AC DOMINO/ DOMINO/ **FRIDERICO CHRISTIANO**/ REGIO POLONIARVM MAGNIQVE DVCATVS LI-/ THVANIAE PRINCIPI ELECTORATVS SAXONICI HI-/REDI DVCI SAXONIAE IVLIAE CLIVIAE MONTIVM ANGRIAE/ ET WESPHALIAE LANDGRAVIO THVRINGIAE MARCHIONI MISNIAE ET SVPERIORIS INFERIORISVE LVSATIAE COMITI PRINCIPALI/ HENNEBERGICO COMITI MARCAE RAVENSBERGAE BARBYAE ET/ HANOVIAE DYNASTAE IN RAVENSTEIN CET./ DOMINO SVO CLEMENTISSIMO/NEC NON/ SERENIXXIMAE PRINCIPI AC DOMINAE/ DOMINAE/ **MARIAE ANTONIAE**/ DIVI CAROLI VII. AVGVSTI FILIAE VTRIVS-OVE BAVARIAE ET SVPERIORIS PALATINATVS/ DVCI CET./ DOMINAE SVAE CLEMENTISSIMAE/ **CONNVBIVM AVGVSTVM**/ NVPER CEMEBRATVM/ ACADEMIA LIPSIENSIS/ D. X. OCTOBR. A. R. G. MDCCXXXXVII/ IN TEMPLO ACADEMICO/ DEVOTISSIMO CVLTV

GRATVLABITVR/ DECENTER INVITAT/ **EIVS RECTOR.**

Notes: Dlb call number: Hist. Sax. C 306

Wrapped in coppered paper. Inside cover has marbled paper. 7 x 10.5 in. Printed source. On page X, it mentions that Friedrich Christian's Arcadian name is : "Lusatio Argiraeo". Other people mentioned in here include J. Gottsched, Graf Wackerbarth, the Princesses Maria Anna and Maria Amalia. Also contains some text in Greek (Page XIII).

1748

> ODE/an die / Durchlauchtigste/Armelinda/Talea,/ [KÖB stamp]/bey/Ihrer Aufnahme/in die/ Akademie der Arkader/ zu Rom. (Lips. [Leipzig], 1748)

Notes: Dlb call number Hist. Sax. C 1668m.

Fol 3r contains an engraving of Maria Antonia surrounded by the attributes of Minerva: Shield, spear, helmet. Two engraver's signaturess: on left, Bloßing del; on right: Bornigeroth Sc. Wrapped in gold/copper (a little green around the gills in spots) paper, approx. 4" x 6". Inside cover sheets red, blue yellow white marbled paper. Printed source. Old German font. Last page (recto) has a footnote: *Siehe den VI Band des Büchersaals der schönen Wissenschaften und freyen Künste, im I Stücke, auf der 3ten und folgenden Seite, allwo ein französishes Gedicht dieser erhabenen Dichterinn, bekannt gemachet worden. Es führet den Titel: Sentimens d'une Ame penitente, sur le Pseaume, *Miserere*, und ist ganz in Kupfer gestochen.

> Als/Ihro Königl. Hoheit/ Maria Antonia,/Königliche Chur-Printzeßin,/ Hertzogin zu Sachsen [&c]./ Der gewöhn-lichen jährlichen großen Weinlese/ in der Königlichen/ Hofe=Lößnitz/ den 16. Octobr. 1748./ In/ Hoher Perso,/

Zum ersten mahle/ beyzuwohnen, aus besondern Gnacen geruheten,/ Wollte/Dersoselbe/ Durchlauchtigst=Hohe Gegenwart/ mit einigen gebundenen Zeile/ in tiefster Unterhänigkeit verehren/ Die Hof=Lößnitz. /[Line] Dresden, gedruckt bey der verwitt. Königln. Hof=Buchdr. Stößelin.

Notes: Dlb call number: Hist Sax. C 318.

Wintzer=Lied,/Welches/bey erster hoechsten Gegenwart/ Ihro Koenigin. Hoheit/ Der Durchlauchtigsten / Frauen/ Marien Antonien, /vermaehlte/ Koenigl. Saechsis. Chur=Printzeßin, und in hoechster Gesellschaft/ Dero Herrn Gemahls/ Des / Koenigl. Chur=Printzens, / Wie auch / Printzen Xaveri und Carls/ Koenigl. Hoheiten Hoheiten Hoheiten,/ Wehrend der Weinlese in der Koenigl. Hof=Loeßnitz) unter Anfuehrung/ eines Frantzoesischen Wintzers von 6. Jungen Wintzern und 6. Jungen Win=/ tzer=Maedgens, tantzend um die Tafel herum, unterhaenigst abgesungen worden, / am 16. October 1748. /[KÖB stamp]

Notes: Dlb call number: Hist Sax. C. 1163.

Burgundy fabric over cardboard cover. German song text.

Festeggiandos i/ il / Felicissimo Giorno Natalizio/ di / Maria Antonia Principessa Reale / di Sassonia./ il Dì 18 Luglio 1748. [KPMS and SLB stamps).

Notes: Dlb (Mus 3096-L-2). Music by Schürer. In an Italian hand. Cover is coppery paper, inside of which is backed by white paper with a purple, red and yellow floral pattern. Watermarks are a Fleur-de-lys and IV.

Dedication reads: Altezza!/ Stimo, che non correrò la taccia di temerario, se a tanto popolo mi unisco anch'io per celebrar come posso, se non quanto dovrei, il fortunato Giorno del suo Glorioso Natale, offerendole questa piccola Can sarà cantata in quest'oggi da miei Tedeschi Scolari, quali sotto la mia condotta aspirano, uniti al Maestro di farsi strada al di lei alto Patrocinio. La Singolar Clemenza di Vostra Altezza, ch'è stata quella che mi ha dato il coraggio, mi fa sperare un gradimento generoso. Tanto io, quanto il compositore della Musica Gio. Georgio Schürrer (sic), ed i Cantanti, coll'armonia delle note, averebbemo ardito spiegar l'armonia delle tante Virtudi, che l'Altezza Vostra adornano. Mà come l'accordo di queste è perfetto, e le note saran difettose, così la supplico accogliendone benignamente il solo pensiero degnarsi di farce dono del suo penignissimo compatimento, ed a Vostra Altezza m'inchino con profondissima umiliazione. / Di Vostra Altezza./ umilissimo servitore/ D. Biagio Campagnari.

1749

Knoblauch, Johann George. *Das Salz am Hofe, / An/ Ihro /Koenigl. Hoheit/ gebohrner Kaeyserlichen und vermaehlter/ Chur=Princeßin / zu Sachsen, / hohen / Nahmens= /und / Vermaehlungs=Fest, / den 13. Jun. 1749. / Bey dem/ Koenigl. Pohln. Und Churfuerstl. Saechß. Hofe / zu Dreßden, / allerun-terhaenigst præsentiret /* von / Johann George Knoblauch. [Line] *Zittau,/ gedruckt bey Johann Gottlieb Nicolai.*

Notes: Dlb call number: Coll. Diss. A 244, 6.

13" x 12" (approx.) folded in two to make four pages. A poem, in German, to Maria Antonia on the occasion of her name and marriage celebration.

Pasquini, Giovanni Claudio. ETRENNE POETIQUE./ I LAMENTI D'ORFEO/ COMPONIMENTO DRAMMATICO/ CONSAGRATO/ A / SUA ALTEZZA REALE/ ED/ ELETTORALE/ *LA PRINCIPESSA*/ MARIA ANTONIA VALPURGA, TRA GLI ARCADI/ ERMELINDA TALEA/ DA TRIGENO MIGONITIDIO PASTORE/ ARCADE. FU POSTA IN MUSICA) DAL SIG.ʳ GIOVANNI RISTORI,/ COMPOSITORE DI CAMERA DI S.R.M./ [line] / *DRESDA* / L'ANNO M DCC XLIX. NELLA STAMPERIA/ DELLA VEDOVA HARPETER. [KÖB STAMP]

Notes: Dlb Call number: Hist Sax C. 1164

Red leather cover, stamped with gold. Coppered paper as endpages. Fol 1v reads : *CANTANO:* / *C*ALLIOPE, una delle Muse./ La Sigᵃ. Rosa Pavona./ ORFEO, Filiuolo della Medesima. / La Sigᵃ. Regina Mingotti. / L'Azione si finge alle falde del Monte Parnaso. Watermark: two crossed swords

Ristori, Giovanni Alberto. I LAMENTI D'ORFEO. (Handwritten calligraphy on title page as follows:) I Lamenti d'Orfeo/ Festa di Camera consagrata alle Glorie Auguste/ di/ Ermelinda Talea. / Patroncinio, e Decoro d'Arcadia / Poesia del Sig.ʳᵉ Ab:ᵗᵉ Gio. Claudio Pasquini d:ᵗᵒ Trigenio Migonitidio/ Pastore Arcade./ Musica di Gio. Alberto Ristori 1749. / [KPMS stamp: crown within oval, very faded.]

Notes: Dlb Call number (from the Musik Abteilung): Mus. 2455-L-3

Watermark for Vander ley (shield with hunting horn & a very faded V underneath).

Brown leather cover, stamped gold border. Red, yellow, green, white zig-zag marbled paper inside cover. Gilded paper.

1754

Porpora, Nicolo. *Sonate XII de Viol e Basso*

Notes: Dlb call number (from Musikabteilung): Mus 2417-R-1.

The title page reads: [inside an 18th century border] Sonate XII. Di Violino, e Basso / Dedicate / A S. A. R. La Principessa Elettorale di Sassonia / Maria Antonia Walburga / di Baviera / da / Niccolò Porpora / Maestro di Cappella di S. M. il Re di Polonia / [18th c decoration] / In Vienna d'Austria. 1754. (KPMS stamp)

Outside the border, SLB stamp. This page is neatly hand-calligraphed, not engraved. The music is engraved. At end "Nicolai Sculps: Vieñe"

All pages are dog-eared on bottom right corner and darkened in same place due to use.

Dark brown leather cover with gold stamped border. Flower decoration in corners, and four flowers in the shape of a diamond in the center of the covers (front and back). On spine is a red leather label, "Porpora / 12 sonate / di violine". The covers have slightly separated from the spine at the top and bottom. Inside cover is a red marbled paper. All pages gilt-edged. IEP with crowned double headed eagle watermark on front cover sheet. Same as countermark on back.

Dedication reads: (inside an 18th-century border] Reale, et Elettorale Altezza. / Le dodici sonate di Violino e Basso (o sia di Cimbalo e Violincello) che alla Reale et Elet= / =torale Altezza Vostra in umil tributo io presento, Non sono di Sua ragione per debito solamente di / quella gloriosa servitù, che a si gran segno mi onora; ma sono altresi dovute a quella profonda sua intel= / =ligenza delle belle arti, che in ciascheduno è lodevole, Et in una sua pari è portento. Conoscerà L'A. V. R. Et E. Che con questa specie di decisione dimostrativa io mi sono Studiato di mettere in pace le più colte Na= / =zioni d'Europa cosi mal concordi fra loro sulla preferenza dell'antica e della moderna Musica, dell'Ita= / =liana e della Francese. Ravviserà nelle prime sei scritte a doppia corda (e specialmente in quella delle Me= / =desime, in cui ò [sic] fatto particolar uso de' tre generi diatonico, enarmonico, e coromatico) che nella rigorosa / osservanza de' precetti possono trovar di che compiacersi ancora i più zelanti seguqci dell'ornato moderno / stile: E che i severi custodi all'incontro della rigida antichità non incontreranno di che rincrescersi nella / vivace, e capricciosa mistura d'antico di Moderno; d'Italiano, e di Francese che regna nelle altre sei. / E se mai, cedendo la mia lunga esperienza agli angusti limiti del mio talento, non mi fosse riuscito di / provare abbastanza, che dissentono per la diversità dè difetti, ma si accordano nell'unità del buono tutti i secoli e tutte le Nazioni; sarà sempre per me soprabbondante pregio dell'opera la sospirato oppor= / =tunità che mi procuro di publicarmi con la più riverente Sommissione. / Di V. A. R. Et E. / [KPMS stamp] / L'umilissimo et Ossequiosissimo Attual Servitore / Niccolo Porpora.

1757

Der/über die höchstbeglückte/Hohe Niederkunfft [sic] / Ihro Königlichen Hoheit/ Der Durchlauchtigsten Frau,/ FRAU/ Marien Antonien Walpurgis,/ Königlicher/ Chur=Printzeßin in Sachsen [&c]./ erfreuete / Chur=Sächßische Helicon / wird vorgestellet/ alhier in Dresden / am 26, Sept. Ann. 1757, / von einem/ In Gott Ohne Sorge, / [line]/ DRESDEN, / gedruckt bey der verwitw. Königl. Hofbuchdr. Stößelin, und / deren Adj. Johann Carl Krausen. [KÖB stamp].

Notes: Dlb call number: Hist. Sax. C 319

Approx. 7" x 11". Green fabric covered. Inside cover is golden/ copper paper covered with flowers that are different colors: orange, purple, green, white, pink, yellow. Printed source. Gilded edges. 36 pp.

1758

von Runckel, Dorothe Heinriette. *An dem/ Hohen Geburts=Feste / Der Durchlauchtigsten Fürstinn und Frau, / FRAU/ Maria Antonia,/ Vermählter/ Königlicher Churprinzeßinn zu Sachßen [&c.]/ gebohrner Kayserlichen Prinzeßinn/ aus Bayern, / Wolte ihre unterthänigsten / Glückwünsche / in tiefster Ehrfurcht / darlegen/ Dorothe Heinriette von Runckel./ [line]/ Den 18. Julii 1758. / [line]/ Dreßden, gedruckt bey Johann Willhelm Harpetern. /* [KÖB stamp]

Notes: Dlb call number: Hist Sax. C 323

6" x 10". White fabric covered paper cover. Inside lining is light blue fabric. Addresses Maria Antonia as the mother of the people and talks about her releasing them from Hunger and Want.

Otto, Johann Gottlob. *Der Durchlauchtigsten Fürstin/ und Frau Frau/ Marien Antonien Walpurgis, / Königlicher Churprintsessin in Sachsen, / gebohrner / Kaijserlicher und Churprintsessin/ in Bayern, / gratuliret hierdurch / zu Höchstderoselben / am 18.ten Julü Anno 1758. / hinswiederum glücklichst erlebsen / Geburtstage / [?] / [....devotes..??]] [??] / Johann Gottlob Otto. / [????] / Secretarius / [...] /* [KÖB stamp]

Notes: Dlb call number: Hist. Sax. C. 325

Handwritten title page. Gold paper cover backed by silver raised design. Contains the text to arias and recitatives sung by the princesses Christina, Elisabeth and Cunigunda to Maria Antonia. All in German.

COMPONIMENTO/ PER MUSICA/ DA CANTARSI / IL DI 13 GIUGNO 1758/ PER/ FESTEGGIARE/ IL NOME/ DI / ERMELINDA TALEA /P. A. / [ship in harbor & KÖB stamp]/ [line] /DRESDA, MDCCLVII. / [line] / Nella Stamperia Regia per la Vedova Stössel, e'l suo aggiunto Giov. Carlo Krause.

Notes: Dlb call number: Hist Sax. C. 1181, 12.

Printed paper cover, yellow flowers on a red and white background.

In pencil on the bottom (in an 18th-century hand?) is: Éxecuté à l'occasion de la dite fête par LL.AA.RR. Les Dames les Princesses Royles Elisabet et Cunigonde, accompagnées par LL. AA. RR les Princes Albert et Clement.

1760

von Töehern, Johann Christoph. *Unterhänigist Devotester mit Rosen, / Gezierter Gluckwunsch. / an /Ihro Königl. Hoheit/ Die Durchlauchtigste Cron und Chur=/Prinzeßin aus sachsen / als / Höchstdieselbe in der Angenemsten Früch= / lings Zeiten 15.[m] Junÿ 1760. Inhrs[????]/ Dero Glor[???] Heill: Nahmens Tag / Feyrlichst Celebriert / Diemüthigist Præsentiret / Von/ Johann Christoph von Töehern/Jur: [?????] Cande.*

Notes: Dlb call number: Hist. Sax. C 1165m

Wrapped in Wedgwood blue silk fabric, closed with ribbons of the same and of white fabric (on the front cover, one is missing, but presumably was white, since the top one is blue, and on the back cover, the remaining two are white [top] and blue [bottom]). Inside cover has marbled paper: red, blue, yellow, white, some green.

Handwritten source. 5.5" x 5.75". Quite ornate, often beautiful writing. Fol 2r has a drawing of a lion among a bunch of hills with four roses. It's beautifully colored: the sky is blue with white clouds, the field and hills are green, the roses are red, the lion is golden. The mountains in the distance are blue. The whole thing is framed in copper paint/ink. The entire page is bordered in red. All pages are bordered in red, and towards the end, some of the text is written in red ink.

1762

An dem / Hoechsten Geburth=Fest / Ihro Koenigl. Hoheit, Maria Antonia, Koenigl. Prinzeßin von Pohlen und Litthauen, / Herzogin zu Sachsen, u. Geb. Kaiserl. Prin= / zeßin von Ober-= und Nieder=Bayern, u. / unsrer gnaedigsten Churprinzeßin, / wird / von der helden=Muse ein poetischer Prologus auf dem hiefigen / Theatro im Zwinger, in allerunterhaenigster Demuth und Vene- / ration vorgestellet, und Hoechst Deroselben dediciret, / genannt: / Der von redlich=gesinnten Herzen, in / den Tempel der Weißheit entzuendete Weyrauch. [Line] 1762. / [KÖB stamp] Notes: Dlb call number: Hist Sax. C 1166

Plain cover, backed by silvered paper.

1763

Marainville, Comte de. *Détail d'un Divertissement, donné le dernier jour de Carneval 1763 à S. A. R. Madame la Princesse Electorale de Saxe.* (Dresden: Walther, 1763).

Notes: for more, see Part 3, below.

Martini, Giambattista. DUETTI DA CAMERA / CONSAGRATI / All'Altezza Reale Elettorale di / MARIA ANTONIA / DI BAVIERA / PRINCIPESSA ELETTORALE / DI SASSONIA / DA FR. GIAMBATISTA MARTINI DE'

MINORI CONVENTUALI / Accademico nell' Instituto delle Scienze, e Filarmonico.

Notes: from Staatsbibliothek Berlin, Amalien-Bibliothek, call number Am B 444.

1765

[in an 18th-century border:]

Ueber die / beglückts Ankunft / des / Durchlauchtigsten Fürsten und Herrn / HERRN / Friedrich Augusts / Herzogs zu Sachsen, Jülich, Cleve, Berg, Engern und Westphalen, des Heil. Röm. Reichs Erzmarschalls und Churfürsten, [&c.] / wie auch der / Durchlauchtigsten Fürstinn und Frauen / FRAUEN / Marien Antonien / Verwitweten Königlichen Prinzeßinn in Pohlen und Litthauen, / Churfürstinn zu Sachsen, [&c.] / und des / Durchlauchtigsten Fürsten und Herrn / HERRN / Xaverii / Königl. Prinzen in Pohlen und Litthauen, Herzogs zu Sachsen, / Jülich, Cleve, Berg, Engern und Westphalen, [&c.] / der Chur Sachsen Administratoris / bezeigen ihre devoteste Freude / Sämmtliche auf der Universität Leipzig Studierende.

Notes: Dlb call number: Hist. Sax. C 400, 15n

The royal and electoral family had a very close relationship to the city of Leipzig. This appears to be the libretto to a work sung to honor Maria Antonia, Friedrich August, and Prince Administrator Xavier. At end, the date: 1765.

Zu / Den Allerhöchsten NahmensTage / Ihr: Königlichen Hoheit / Der / Durchlauchtigsten Cron und Chur=Fürstin. / MARIA ANTONIA / [the rest is handwritten] 13. Juny 1765./ [both KPMS stamps]

Notes: Dlb call number: Hist. Sax. C 400, 30

Cover is coppered paper with an embossed design. 7.5" x 12".

1766

> Clodius, Christian August. *Ode auf die Wiederherstellung Ihrer Königlichen Hoheit der Churfürstinn...* (Leipzig: Breitkopf, 1766).
>
> Notes: Dla Sc 1012

> Gottsched, Johann Christian. *Thalestris, Königinn der Amazonen aus dem vortrefflichen italienischen Singespiele Ihrer Königlichen Hoheit der unvergleichlichen Ermelinde Thalea in ein Deutsches Trauerspiel verwandelt* (Zwickau: Christian Lebrecht Stielern, 1766).

1767

> Bach, W.F. *Concerto / per il Cembalo / con Violini, Viola, e Basso / di / Guglielmo Friedeman / Bach*
>
> Dlb (Mus. 2990-0-1,1 & 2)

There is a copy of this on microfilm at Harvard. It is something that was sent to Maria Antonia. The copyist is thought to have been from Dresden. The letter after it dates from 1767. The letter to her is in German, and has been put into modern type and published in Falck's *Wilhelm Friedemann Bach* (Leipzig, 1919), p. 43. Interesting things about the harpsichord part: penciled-in figuring for the bass in the last half of the score. Wax drops on back imply at least one use. Someone has put in some measure counts in some areas in pencil. KPMS and KOP stamps on all parts and letter. Watermark (for the letter) is a hunting horn in a shield opposite the word "HALLE."

Ferrandini, A. *XII Duetti / del Maestro Ferrandini fatti / per il divertimento di S. A. R. l'Elettrice Madre di Sassoni / a dì 9 Luglio 1769*

Dlb (3054-L-1)

29.5 cm (w) x 22 cm (h). Bound in blue lined paper. Watermark is Fleur de lys in a shield surmounted by a crown, with the number 4 underneath. Handwriting seems Italian. No first name, therefore attribution to Antonio rather than Giovanni is unclear. However, the handwriting does not look like that associated with G. Ferrandini's works. All AABB, double soprano duets, on pastoral texts (Nice & Clori etc). 35 pp.

1772

ADUNANZA / TENUTA DAGLI ARCADI / Nella Villa Sciarra / Ad onore di Sua Altezza Reale / MARIA ANTONIA / WALBURGA DI BAVIERA / Elettrice Vedova Di Sassonia / Fra le Pastorelle Acclamate / ERMELINDA TALEA/ [KÖB STAMP] / [putto playing a panpipe, sitting on grass] / IN ROMA MD CCLXXII. / [lines] / Per Arcangelo Casaletti.

Notes: Dlb call number Hist Sax. C. 1667.

Sonnets by different members of the Arcadian Academy for Maria Antonia on the occasion of her departure from Rome.

[within and 18th-century border:]
VARI / **COMPONIMENTI** / PER MUSICA / DI **ERMELINDA TALEA** / REALE PASTORELLA / ARCADE / Calamo ludimus. / [printer's mark] / IN MONACO DI BAVIERA. / [lines] / Nella Stampiera del Eletorale Academia

/ 1772. [Stamp: "A." surmounted by a crown. Monogram of Anton, perhaps?]

Notes: Dlb call number (Musikabteilung) MT 2309 Rara

Old call number on inside front cover sheet, in ink: Princip. Quart r9r f. In pencil above that, another call number: Sax. Princ. Op.586.

19th-century (?) cardboard cover has the Saxony shield surmounted by a crown embossed in gold on the spine. In a green box is written on the spine: Vari/ Componimenti/ di / E. T. R. P [sic]. The cover is brown marbled paper.

On inside back cover, in pencil is written: "Schlossbibl. Moritzburg (Teile)/ 3 Ex./ 1. Ex.: Lit. Ital. D 313 d / 2.Ex.: Lit. Ital. D. 313 f"

Contents otherwise identical to copies at Harvard and in Munich.

1773

Riminese Accademico Filarmonico et al. *Il secolo vendicato. Dramma musicale da cantarsi nel publico teatro di Rimine l'anno 1773...alla reale altezza di Maria Antonia Walburga di Baviera.* (Cesena, 1773).

Notes: Dla call number Sc 1006

1774

Eximeno y Pujades, Antonio. **DELL'ORIGINE** / E DELLE REGOLE / **DELLA MUSICA** / COLLA STORIA DEL SUO PROGRESSO, / DECADENZA E RINNOVAZIONE. / OPERA / **DI D. ANTONIO EXIMENO** / FRA I PASTORI ARCADI ARISTOSSENO MEGA REO / DEDICATA / ALL' AUGUSTA REAL PRINCIPESSA / **MARIA ANTONIA VALLBURGA** / DI BAVIERA / ELETTRICE VEDOVA DI SASSONIA / FRA LE PASTORELLE ARCADI / ERMELINDA TALEA. /

[Arcadian seal: panpipes surrounded by wreath and fauns, surmounted by the words GLI ARCADI] / IN ROMA MDCCLXXIV. / NELLA STAMPIERIA DI MICHEL' ANGELO BARBIELLINI / NEL PALAZZO MASSIMI. / [ornate line] / CON FACOLTÀ DE' SUPERIORI.

Notes: US: CAh call number: Isham Mus 287.75. Available in a modern reprint (Hildesheim & New York: G. Olms, 1983).

1775

[Under an engraving which shows Arlequino holding up a banner with the Bavarian and Saxon Arms:] Ausführliche Nachricht / von dem / prächtigen Schützenauszug / und / Haupt=und Ehrenchießen / welches / in allhiesiger Haupt=und Residenzstadt auf der gewöhn-lichen / Hauptschießstatt / an dem/höchsterfreulichsten Namensfeste / Ihre königlichen Hochheit / der verwittibten Frauen Frauen Churfürstinn von Sachsen / Antonia,/ [lines] von / Franz Hueber, / churbajerischen Kammerdiener und Weingastgeb zum römischen König / allhier den 12ten Brachmonat 1775. In tiefester Ehrfurct gegeben, und / den 15ten ejusd. Mit allseitigen vergnügen geendiget worden. / [lines] / München, gedruckt in der Vötterischen Hof= und Landschaftsbuchdruckerey.

Notes: Dlb call number: Hist. Bavar. 180, 30. Details a shooting contest.

1780 and after

> AD / IVSTA FVNEBRIA / PRINCIPI REGIAE / GLORIOSISSIMAE MEMORIAE / MATRI PATRIS PATRIAE / **MARIAE ANTONIAE** / CRAS HORA X. MATVTINA / IN TEMPLO ACADEMICO / SOLEMNITER AC RITE / / *PATRES ACADEMIAE* / PROCERES REI PVBLICAE / AC / GENEROSISSIMOS HUMANISSIMOSQVE CIVES / INVITAT / RECTOR / ACADEMIAE VITEMBERGENSIS / BENIAMIN GOTTLIB LAURENTIVS / BODEN / PROFESSOR POESEOS ORDINARIVS

Notes: Dlb call number: Hist Sax. C. 1168. 6.5" x 7.5"

Marbled paper cover. Stamp of Saxony on fol 1r. In two parts: Part I, 9 leaves. Part II, 4 leaves.

> Part II begins with: LESSVS FERALIS / ANTE ET POST / ORATIONEM / GLORIOSISSIMAE MEMORIAE / PRINCIPIS REGIAE / **MARIAE ANTONIAE** / OPTIMAE OPTIMI FILII PARENTIS / IN / AEDE ACADEMICA VITEMBERGENSI / PVBLICE RECITATAM / HABITVS (stamp of KÖB]

1782

> IN REDITV FELICI / OPTIMORVM SAXONIAE PRINCIPVM / FRIDERICI
> CHRISTIANI / ET / MARIAE ANTONIAE / REDEVNTEM FELICITATEM / PIE GRATVLATVR PATRIAE / [line] CHRISTIANVS AVGVSTVS
> CLODIVS / [line] A.D.XXX. IAN. CI[back. C]I[back C] CCLXII / [KÖB STAMP.]

Notes: Dlb call number: Hist. Sax. C. 1181, 14m

At end "LIPSIAE/EX OFFICINA BREITKOPFIA"

No date [pre-1750?]

Ferrandini, Gio. de. *Arie [24 à Soprano con strom]*

Dlb (Mus 3037-1-6, 1 & 2 & 6a)

Notes: Red leather covers. The decoration on the spine is very similar to that of "30 Arias." Gold stamped borders around the edges. On spine, white paper label, with gold writing within a gold border, "Arien / Ferrandini."

Inside covers, marbled paper. Gilded edges.

On cover: No: XXX. [Book two, No: XXXI.] / [in gold, in a golden border in the middle top of the cover] ARIE / DEL SIG: GIO: FERRANDINI

The dedication (in book one) reads as follows: "Serenissima Altezza Reale~ / Se la tenue mia abilità corrisponder potesse all'immenso, e vivo desiderio, che è sempre nudrito di conciliarmela a perfettione, certo si è, che dovrei stimarmi veramente felice: Qualunque non dimeno Ella siasi, benedico quel giorno, che cominciai ad impiegarla in Esercizio del Nobilissimo Genio di **V. A. R.** Consolandomi all'estremo, che abbia Ella sputo illustrarla in guisa, che nel tempo medesimo sian da tutti compatite le mie debotezze, ed ammirate le di lei sapientissime e Virtuose Maniere. Quindi è, che con lieto Animo prendo l'ardire di umiliarle questi due Libri di nuove Arie da me composte espressamente per L'A. V: Reale, supplicandola con profondissimo ossequio a volersi degnare di gradirli con quella generosa Magnanimità, con cui in ogni riscontro mi a' onorato di autenticarmi la sua Clemenza; E raccomandandomi in tanto alla sua Sovrana Protettione, col più subordinato rispetto mi dico sino all'ultimo Periodo di mia vita. / Di vostra Altezza Serenissima Reale. / [in a paragraph on the bottom, right hand side] Umilissimo, e Subordinatissimo / Servitore Giovanni Ferrandini / Consigliere è Direttore della Musica / di Camera di Sua A:ᶻᵃ S:ᵐᵃ E:ˡᵉ di Baviera.

Basso part missing for XXXI, but Vln 1, Vln 2, Alto Viola parts there for both.

Part 3: Assorted musical Maria Antonia-associated works

DETAIL / D'UN / DIVERTISSEMENT, / DONNÉ LE DERNIER JOUR DE CARNAVAL / 1763. / A S.A.R. / MADAME LA PRINCESSE / ELECTORALE DE SAXE, / PAR / Mr. LE COMTE / DE MARAINVILLE / brigadier des Armées de S. M. Très-Chretienne, / Envoïé à l'Armée Impériale en Saxe. / [Branches] / [lines] / DRESDE, / Chez GEORGE CONRAD WALTHER, / Libraire du Roi. / 1763.

Notes: Dlb (MT 1620, 1 Rara)

This is a verbal description, with some music, of the celebration. Mentions dances. Has the MA personal stamp on the title page, as well as the KPMS double stamps. Underneath the oval stamp, is the stamp "Doublette." which means that this copy was probably sold off in the 19ᵗʰ century, then bought back by SLUB in the 20ᵗʰ century. This copy also belonged to the Stadtbibliothek at one time. The SLB stamp is upside down, but otherwise intact in the lower right hand corner.

This same work exists in manuscript (Mus 3096-1-1). It contains music by Schürer.

[Cantata for Maria Antonia]

Notes: Dlb (Mus 1-F-49, 4-14; 4-18; 4-21)

The card says: "[= vermutl. f. 2. S (Clori, Egle) u. Orch. u. zus. gesetzt aus Arien verschiedener Komponisten u. verbindenden Reditativen (sempl. und accomp.). Verf. des Pasticcios mich erm, genannte Arien komponisten: Bernasconi, Galuppi; die Bestimmung f. Maria Antonia geht aus der mehrfachen Anspielung des Textes auf <<Ermelinda>> hervor. Gesamt umfang noch nicht festgestellt.]"

Appears to be in a Dresden hand, and it does play with Maria Antonia's Arcadian name. Andrea Bernasconi was connected to both Munich and Dresden. See Appendix 3.

[Cantata for Maria Antonia]

Notes: Dlb (Mus 1-F-49, 4-6)

"1775. In Padova. Del Sigl. Michiele Mortellari." written on cover page. An aria for Soprano, horns and oboes in A. First line: "Ombra fedele tornerò a rivederti".

Cantata for Friedrich Christian

Notes: Dlb (Mus 2686-J-1)

Written by "Gio. Domenico Bonlini Nobile Veneto." for Friedrich Christian's name day. The poem is written out separately. The music paper has the three crescents watermark on the music sheets, and a W surmounted by a crown on the remaining cover sheet. Badly water-damaged.

Music by Johann Schürer for the Saxon Royal Family

Nel Felicissimo Giorno del / glorioso Nome / della / SACRA REALE MAESTA / di / AUGUSTO III^{ZO} / Rè di Pollonia, ed Elettore di Sassonia, etc: / CANTATA / à tre Voci sotto li nomi Pastorali / di / Nice, Dorisbe, e Filli.

Notes: Dlb (Mus 3096-L-1). No date. Watermarks are a W on the front cover sheet, and star or flower on the back cover sheet.

Brown leather cover with gold embossed border. Pages are marbled on the edges. Scored for three sopranos (Maria Antonia, Cunigunde and Elisabeth, though it could also be for Christine, Cunigunde and Elisabeth to sing). Opening line: "Sù compagne meco liete/ risvegliate il vostro cor/ ecco il di se nol sapete/ dell'Augusto Genitor." This line is sung by Nice; it is the opening of a duet between Nice and Dorisbe. The cantata closes with a Chorus (3 sopranos), "Viva il nostro Augusto." No KPMS or other stamps.

Missa / ad / Sanctum Antonium de Padua, / quam / in gloriosissimo die onomastico / Serenissimae Principis Electoralis. / Mariae Antoniae Wallprugae [sic] / solenniter producebat / [KPMS stamp] / Dresdae 13 Juny / 1763 / Joannes Georgius Schürer

Notes: D: Dlb (Mus 3096-D-1).

There is a series of six of these masses to Maria Antonia's patron saint (Mus 3096-D-1 thru 6). This one (1763) is the only one in a major key. The rest are in minor. The first is dated 1758, there's nothing for 1759, then one each year: 1760, 61, 62, 63, 64.

Bound in brown leather, with gold stamped border. On spine label "No. 77."

Part 4: Contemporary Articles

1755

Dreßdenischer Merkwürdigkeiten, April 1755

Notes: Dlb Eph hist

20 April 1755: The Hof (Court), including Friedrich Christian, Maria Antonia, Princes Xaver and Clemens, travel from Hubertusburg to Leipzig.

Journal Étranger

Notes: Dlb: Eph. Hist. 428, Mai 1755

An article on pp 128-137 contains a summary of the action of *Trionfo* as published by Beritkopf.

1756

Journal Étranger

Notes: Dlb: Eph. Hist. 428, Jan 1756

p 239: "AIRS DE MUSIQUE./ Mon prédécesseur a eu la gloire d'être le premier François qui ait rendu un hommage public aux talens de la PRINCESSE ROYALE DE POLOGNE ET ELECTORALE DE SAXE. Il fit dans le JOURNAL de Mai 1755 p. 128, l'extrait du TRIOMPHE DE LA FIDELITE', Drame Pastoral en trois Actes, que cette Muse auguste a composé en vers Italiens, qu'elle a mis en Musique, & qui a été exécuté sur le Théâtre de ses petits appartemens. M. L'Abbé *Prévot* promit d'en donner quelques Ariettes. Nous avons l'avantage de remplir oujourd'hui ses engagemens, & de répondre à l'honneur que nous a fait la Princesse de choisir par préférence notre JOURNAL, pour faire part au Public des heureuses productions de son génie. / Voici les paroles des AIRS placés à la fin de ce Volume. *Chloris* dit à *Nice:*"

There follows the text to the aria, *Si sperar tu sola puoi* in Italian, with a French translation underneath. The score of the aria is printed at the end of the volume.

1763

Dreßdenischer Merkwürdigkeiten, Sept. 1763.

Notes: Dlb Eph hist

Part 5: Catalogs

> [No author]. *Catologo de Libri Numerati Musicali d[e] S[on] A[ltesse] R[oyale] M[aria] A[ntonia] D[ux] de B[avaria].* (after 1746).

Dlb Bibl. Arch Hb 787 e (Musikabteilung)

> [No author]. *Catalogus, von Ihro Königliche Hoheit der weÿland Durchlauchtigsten, Fürstin und Frau Frau Maria Antonia, verwittibten Chufürstin zu Sachsen, gebohrnen Römisch Kaÿserlichen Prinzessin und Herzogin in Ober- und Nieder-Bayern, Bibliotheck nebst denen Preissen, zum XXIsten Capitel des Haupt-Inventarii gehörig.* (Dresden, c. 1780).

Dlb Handschriftenabteilung

Part 6: Selected Collections of Letters from Hauptstaatsarchiv, Dresden (D: Dla)

Loc. 3058: Des Cabinets-Ministers Grafens von Brühl mit dem Cabinets Minister und Oberst-Hof-Meister des Chur-Prinzens Graf von Wackerbarth geführte Correspondenz, Vol I: 1746; Vol II: de Anno 1748; Vol III: de Annis 1749 et 1750; Vol IV: 1753 et 1754.

Loc. 3427: Correspondenz des Grafen von Wackerbarth mit dem Grafen von Manteuffel zu Leipzig 1746-48.

Loc. 382: Hoftheater, Ital. Oper, Ausgaben 1753-56, 1763ff

Loc. 30541. Stipulation die Einrichtung der Secundo-Genitur betr. 1776.

Nachlässe 1. Nr. 2. Com A. B. C. D. E. Briefe an der Kurprinzessin MA an ihrer Mutter Maria Amalia, Gemahlin Kaiser Karls VII. 1736, 1737, 1747-1756

Nachlässe 1. Nr. 15 A. B. An dieselbe von ihrem Gemahl, dem Kurprinzen Friedrich Christian. 2 Kon A. B. No 1-246. 1746/47, 1750.

Nachlässe 1 Nr. 16. Briefe an ... von Kurfuerst Friedrich August II, Koenig von Pohlen. 1736-61, 1763.

Nachlässe 1. Nr. 17. Briefe an ... von der Gemahlin FA II (August III) Maria Josepha. 1744-56.

Nachlässe 1. Nr. 19. Briefe an der Kurprinzessin... von ihrem Schwager, Prinzen Xaver von Sachsen. 1752, 1756, 1758/61, 1769/1773, 1778.

Nachlässe 1. Nr. 28 A B C. Briefe ... Von ihrem Sohn Koenig Friedrich August. (Com C hat zwei Schreiben MA undatiert an FA von der... Prinzen Xaver). 1760-62, 1769-1776.

Nachlässe 1 Nr. 62. Briefe von und an Frauen.

Nachlässe 1 Nr. 70 Correspondenz mit Graf Brühl

A: Briefe an Maria Antonia vom 29 Mai 1748 bis 1 Feb 1749 (die briefe Nr 40, 73, 76 sind an dem Prinzen Friedrich Christian gewidmet).

B: Briefe ... von 25 April 1750-15 November 1750.

C: Briefe... Von 2 September bis 10 Dezember 1752.

D: Dgl. Vom 22 Juni 1754 ff.

E: Dsgl. [Of uncertain date].

F: ... 3 Januar 1759 bis 29 Dez 1759. 105

G: ... Von 2 Januar bis 29 Maerz 1760

H. I: 2 April bis Dez 1760.

Nachlässe 1 Nr 72 Briefe von und an Männer

Nachlässe 1 Nr 79 [contains French translations of *Il trionfo della fedeltà, La Conversione di Sant'Agostino,* two fictional works in manuscript from Maria Antonia (*Extrait d'Histoire de S et C* and *Histoire de Madame la Princesse C*), and a letter from Voltaire]

Nachlässe Friedrich Christian

Nr 1: Correspondenz mit August den Starken 1727, 1731, 1732.

Nr. 2: Correspondenz mit Friedrich August II

c: Conv III Schreiben an FC 1744-46, 1748-50, 1752, 1754, 1756-1763.

d: Conv. IV Briefjournal des Kurpr. Friedrich Christian v Sachsen über die Correspondenz mit seinem Vater vom 24 Nov 1757-7 Nov. 1758.

Nr. 4: Königin Maria Josepha

c: 1743-46, 1748-1750, 1752, 1754-1756.

Nr. 10: Maria Antonia. 1746, 1747,5 undatiert.

Nr. 10a: 1 von FC to MA

Nr. 14: Marianne (Maria Anna of Bayern) 1737, 1738-41, 1743-44, 1759, 1762, 1763.

Nr. 15: Maria Amalia of Bayern. 1746-48, 1750-52, 1754-56. Nr. 16: Max Joseph of Bayern. 1747, 1750-52, 1754-57, 1759, 1762-63, 1 undatiert.

Nr. 23: Princess Maria Josepha von Sachsen, Dauphine. 1739-41, 1743, 1744,

1757-1763. 1739. 1 undatiert (c. 1750).

Nr. 27: Prinz Xaver von Sachsen. 1738-40, 1742, 1757-63.

Nr. 28: Prinz Carl von Sachsen. 1750, 1757-63.

Nr. 29: Prinz Albert von Sachsen. 1759-1763.

Nr. 60: Agnesi, Maria Gaetana. 1749.

Nr. 256: Schreiben des Kurprinzen Friedr. Christian v. S an einen sächsischen Geheimrath zu Leipzig... 1750.

K. L.: Dsgl. Von Jahr 1761, Jan bis Dez. No 1-58 intus 1b, und 59-107.

M. N.: Briefe Bruehls 3 Maerz bis Ende Dezember 1762.

O: Dsgl. Januar bis Juli 1763

P: Briefe ohne datum.

R: Briefe MA an Bruehl von dem Jahre 1750 und 1763.

Appendix 3:
Musicians found in
Catalogo dei libri numerati

The following biographical information is drawn primarily from the *New Grove Dictionary of Music and Musicians* (2000).

Abaco: Could be either Evaristo Felice Dall'Abaco (*b* Verona, 12 July 1675; *d* Munich, 12 July 1742) or his son Joseph-Marie-Clément (*b* Brussels, bap. 27 March 1710; *d* Arbizzano di Valpolicella, 31 Aug 1805). More likely the former, although neither is thought of as a composer of vocal music. Evaristo was a cellist and Konzertmeister to Maximilian II Emmanuel, Maria Antonia's grandfather.

Abos, Girolamo (Matteo): (*b* Valetta, 16 Nov 1715; *d* Naples, Oct 1760). Maltese composer and teacher. His principal teachers were probably Gaetano Greco, Francesco Durante, and Gerolimo Ferrara. Served as maestro di cappella at several important Neapolitan churches.

Albertis: Possibly Domenico Alberti (*b* Venice c1710, *d* Rome, 14 Oct 1746), Italian harpsichordist, composer, and singer. Reportedly trained with A. Biffi and A. Lotti. Joined the household of Marquis Giovanni Carlo Molinari in Rome after 1736. Farinelli reportedly admired Alberti's singing.

Battoni: Possibly Giovanni Battista Batoni and possibly a brother of the painter Pompeo Girolamo Batoni (*b* Lucca, 1708; *d* Rome, 1787), who was a contemporary of, and regarded as highly as, Anton Raphael Mengs. Violin sonatas (in manuscript) by a G. B. Battoni may be found in the Národní Muzeum, Prague and Biblioteca Nazionale Braidense, Milan and a collection of fifteen arias for soprano and instruments (also in manuscript) in the Königlichen Privat-Musikaliensammlung, SLUB.[133]

Bernasconi, Andrea: (*b* ?Marseilles, 1706; *d* Munich, 24 Jan 1784). Italian composer. From 1744 to 1753, he was maestro di cappella at the Ospedale della Pietà in Venice. In 1747, he married Maria Josepha Wagele (c1722-1762) in Parma. He trained his stepdaughter, Antonia, in music and helped launch her successful singing career. (Antonia sang in the 1768 production of the unauthorized revision of *Trionfo*. See chapter 7 of the present work.) His appointment as assistant Kapellmeister of vocal music in Munich from 1 August 1753 coincided with the opening of the Residenztheater. On 5 June 1754, he was named music teacher to two of Maria Antonia's sisters, the Princesses **Maria Anna Josepha** and **Josepha Maria**. The Elector **Maximilian III Joseph** also received music lessons from him. Bernasconi was

---

133 Britannica, The Editors of Encyclopaedia. "Pompeo Girolamo Batoni". *Encyclopedia Britannica*, https://www.britannica.com/biography/Pompeo-Girolamo-Batoni. Accessed 23 January 2023.

de Brie, Tim. https://composers-classical-music.com/. Accessed 23 January 2023.

meanwhile appointed electoral councillor. Following Porta's death, Bernasconi was appointed Kapellmeister.

Bertoni, Ferdinando: (*b* Salò, nr Brescia, 15 Aug 1725; *d* Desenzano, nr Lake Garda, 1 Dec 1813). Italian composer. Studied composition with Padre Martini in Bologna. Performances of his operas, especially the comic ones, were produced throughout Europe.

Canaci: Possibly Francesco Baglioni (*fl* 1729-62) known as Carnace or Carnacci. He was a bass, and one of the most popular singers of his day. His popularity was based equally upon his singing and acting abilities.[134] He appeared in comic operas, and in the first collaboration between Galuppi and Goldoni *L'arcadia in Brenta* in 1749 in Venice.

di Capua, Rinaldo: (*b* Capua or Naples c 1705; *d* ?Rome, c1780). Made his opera career in Rome. His satirical opera *La commedia in commedia* was so successful at the Teatro Valle in 1738 that it was repeated in Florence (1741), London (1748), Venice (1749), and Munich (1749), and various versions of it were staged under other titles elsewhere.

Chiarino: Probably Pietro Chiarini (*b* Brescia, early 18th c, *d* ?Cremona, after c1765). His operas were produced at theaters in Venice, Verona, and Genoa from 1738 to 1746. A contemporary of Galuppi, and a collaborator with Goldoni.

Cocchi, Giachino: (*b* ?Naples, 1712, *d* Venice, 11 Sept 1796). Studied with Giovanni Veneziano. Established himself as composer of

---

134 Bucciarelli, pp. 13, 24.

both serious and comic operas in both Naples and Rome, and had an international career that included a position as music director and opera composer to London's Haymarket Theater.

Conti: most likely Nicola Conti (*fl* Naples, 1733-54) who studied with Durante and was later *maestro di musica* of many Neapolitan churches. He wrote several operas but was mainly a composer of sacred music.

Ferrandini, Giovanni Battista: (*b* Venice c1710, *d* Munich 25 Sept 1791). Studied with Antonio Biffi at the Conservatorio dei Mendicanti in Venice before coming to Munich as a boy. (See chapter 4 of the present volume for his connection to Maria Antonia.)

Galuppi, Baldassare: (*b* Burano, nr Venice, 18 Oct 1706; *d* Venice, 3 Jan 1785). Considered a central figure in the development of the *dramma giocoso* and one of the most important mid-18th century *opera seria* composers. Studied with Antonio Lotti. Had a successful career involving positions in London, Venice, Naples, and Rome and commissions in St. Petersburg and Vienna. Long-term collaborator with Carlo Goldoni.

Giaj, Giovanni Antonio: Also spelled Giai or Giay (*b* Turin, 11 June 1690; *d* Turin, 10 Sept 1764). Italian composer. His operas were performed in Turin, Venice, Milan and Rome. Early training under Francesco Fasoli in the Cappella degli Innocenti of the Turin cathedral.

Gluck, Christoph Willibald: (*b* Erasbach, Upper Palatinate, 2 July 1714; *d* Vienna, 15 Nov 1787). Bohemian composer, long in the Habsburg service.

Graun: Most likely Carl Heinrich (*b* Wharenbrück, 1703/4; *d* 8 Aug 1759), who was well known as a composer of operas, cantatas, and sacred vocal works. Appointed court Kapellmeister Crown Prince Frederick of Prussia from 1735.

Hasse, Johann Adolf: (*b* Bergedorf, nr Hamburg, bap 25 Mar 1699; *d* Venice, 16 Dec 1783). His early training included study with Alessandro Scarlatti in Naples, and he wrote many operas and inter-mezzi for the Neopolitan court (and for the Austrian royal family, who ruled there until 1734). Hasse arrived in Dresden for the first time, in 1731, premiering his *Cleofide* on 13 Sept, with his spouse, Faustina Bordoni in the title role. Their contract stipulated that they need be at court only when the King was in residence in Dresden; they were not obliged to travel to Warsaw. Therefore, when not in Dresden, they engaged in performances of his operas throughout Europe. Hasse was appointed Kapellmeister in Dresden under Friedrich August II in 1733 but divided most of this time that year between Vienna and Venice. He continued to move between Italy and Dresden, contributing operas and oratorios to both.

When the Seven Years' War broke out, Hasse and his spouse were given leave to travel, as were most of the musicians at court. He gained permission to visit and to compose music for Naples through Maria Amalia (formerly of Saxony, now Queen of Two Sicilies). He continued to send music to the exiled Elector, who brought what he could of his court to Warsaw. The Hubertusburg Peace in February 1763 meant the return of the King and musicians to Dresden. But his death, and Saxony's greatly reduced economy following this devastating war, meant that the financial support of this court reached its end. Hasse and Bordoni were paid two years' salary and were preparing to leave Dresden when Friedrich Christian died. They stayed an extra few months, and the requiem that Hasse had composed for the father was now performed again for the son. After another payment, they left Dresden for Vienna. Hasse was allowed to continue to use his title of *primo maestro di cappella del re di Polonia ed elettore di Sassonia* on libretti. In Vienna, Hasse continued to build upon the relationship he had developed years earlier with Metastasio. He had become Metastasio's composer of choice. Hasse and Bordoni's final years were spent in Venice.

Jomelli, Niccolò: (*b* Aversa, 10 Sept 1714; *d* Naples, 25 Aug 1774). Considered to be among those who initiated the mid-18th century modifications to singer-dominated Italian opera. Influences included Hasse and Leo. Elected member of the Accademia Filarmonica, and wrote operas for Bologna, Venice, Turin, Ferrara, and Padua. Jomelli was inducted into the **Arcadian Academy** under the name of Anfione Eteoclide shortly before taking up his position of Ober-Kapellmeister at the court of Carl Eugen in Stuttgart.

Lampugnani, Giovanni Battista: (*b* Milan, 1708; *d* Milan, 2 June 1788). Italian composer. His first opera *Candace* was given at the Teatro Regio Ducale, Milan. Several of his operas were frequently performed in London and throughout northern and central Italy (Milan, Venice, Florence, Reggio nell'Emilia, etc.). After 1759, increasingly active as a teacher of singing.

Leo, Leonardo: (*b* 5 Aug 1694; d Naples, 31 Oct 1744). Italian composer and teacher. One of the leading Neapolitan composers of his day, especially of theater and church music.

Maggiore, Francesco: (*b* ?Naples, c1715; *d* ?Netherlands, ?1782). Studied under Durante at the Conservatorio dei Poveri di Gesù in Naples, 1730-35. Composed both comic and serious operas for Venice, Naples, and elsewhere in Italy.

Manna, Gennaro: (*b* Naples, 12 Dec 1715; *d* Naples, 28 Dec 1779). Composer. Nephew of composer Francesco Feo. First opera *Tito Manilo* performed in 1742 in Rome. Appointed maestro di cappella to the city of Naples in 1744, enthusiastic public reception of his seria opera *Achille in Sciro* led to his being sought after outside Naples: by the French ambassador, Saxon court, and theaters in other Italian cities.

Mazzoni, Antonio (Maria): Mazzoni (*b* Bologna, 4 Jan 1717; *d* Bologna, 8 Dec 1785). Italian composer. In 1736 admitted to the Accademia Filarmonica as a tenor, later as a composer. Works of his produced in Lisbon (assisted David Perez in composing two operas for the opening of the new Teatro dos Paços de Ribeira in 1755), and in Italy.

Micheli: Probably Benedetto Micheli (*b* Rome, ?c1700; *d* after 15 Sept 1784). Italian composer, poet, and painter.

Pergolesi, Giovanni Battista: (*b* Iesi, Marche, 4 Jan 1710; *d* Pozzuoli, nr Naples, 16 March 1736). Leading figure in the rise of Italian comic opera in 18th c.

Perez, David: (*b* Naples, 1711; *d* Lisbon, 30 Oct 1778). Italian composer. Family Neapolitan but of Spanish origin. A composer of operas in the *seria* style that were staged throughout Italy and in Vienna and of sacred music. In 1752, became *mestre de capela* to the King of Portugal, a position he held until his death.

Pescetti, Giovanni Battista: (*b* Venice, c1704; *d* Venice, 20 March 1766). Italian composer. Studied with Antonio Lotti, organist at S Marco, Venice.

Porpora, Nicola: (*b* Naples, 17 Aug 1686; *d* Naples, 3 March 1768). Music teacher under title of *maestro* at the Conservatorio di S Onofrio in Naples, primarily known as an opera composer. One of his singing pupils was the castrato Farinelli. His *Damiro e Pitia* was produced in Munich in 1724, and he produced several operas for Venice and Rome in the following years. In 1747, he became singing teacher to **Maria Antonia**. His opera *Filandro* was produced for her birthday, and in April 1748 Porpora was appointed Kapellmeister. He left Dresden in 1752 for Vienna where he continued to teach singing to, among others, Marianne von Martínez, a protegee of Metastasio. Porpora returned to Naples in 1760 as Maestro di cappella at the Conservatorio di S Maria di Loreto.

Porta, Giovanni: (*b* Venice or the Veneto, c1675; *d* Munich, 21 June 1755). Pupil of Francesco Gasparini, thought to have been at Cardinal Ottoboni's court in Rome from 1706 to 1710 where he would have worked with Corelli. Composed operas for Italian theaters, and from 1726 to 1737 was maestro di coro at the Ospedale della Pietà in Venice where he was a colleague of Vivaldi and wrote sacred music for the all-female chorus and orchestra. From 1726 on the roster of the Accademia Filarmonica in Verona. Left Venice in 1737 to accept the position as Hofkapellmeister to the Elector Karl Albrecht in Munich where he remained until his death.

Pulli, Pietro: (*b* Naples, c 1710; *d* 1759 or later). He is named as the Neapolitan *maestro di cappella* in several works. Pulli worked in Naples until at least 1734, thereafter the remainder of his operas were produced in Northern Italy.

Ristori, Giovanni Alberto: (*b* Bologna 1692, *d* Dresden, 7 Feb 1753). Was the son of Tommaso Ristori, a musician and actor and the director of the *commedia* troupe which had been in the service of Saxon Elector Johann Georg III in Dresden. The *commedia* troupe took up permanent residence in Dresden from 1715, under Elector Friedrich August I (King August II of Poland). Giovanni was appointed composer to the Italian theater managed by his father in 1717 and was also made director of the Polish chapel at that same time. This cappella accompanied August II on his journey to Poland, and included Johann Joachim Quantz as oboist and Franz Benda as violinist. In the 1720s, after the Italian opera scandal caused by the King Elector's overeager hiring practices, the Ristoris stayed on at court. Giovanni was responsible for contributing both sacred and secular music for court celebrations in Dresden and in Poland court, together with Johann Heinichen and Jan Dismas Zelenka. During the 1730s, Giovanni spent time in Russia with his father's troupe at the invitation of the Empress Anna Ivanovna.

The later 1730s brought changes in fortune: August the Strong died in 1733 and Giovanni was given the rank of chamber organist. His father retired from the Italian comedy at the age of 75, and *opera seria* took its place as the entertainment form favored by the new monarch, Friedrich August II/August III. This was supported by the hiring and promotion of "il caro Sassone," Johann Adolf Hasse. Ristori continued to compose cantatas and sacred works as well as operas such as *Le fate* (performed 10 Aug 1736) and *Arianna* (7 Oct 1736 at Hubertusburg for the King Elector's birthday). He also continued to write works for use at the Polish court.

His duties as chamber organist meant that he was the one to accompany Maria Amalia to Naples upon her marriage to Charles III, King of Two Sicilies. It was there that he directed the rehearsals and performances of his operas *Temistocle* and *Adriano in Siria*, both to texts by Metastasio, in 1738 and 1739. He returned to Dresden by 1744 and continued to compose masses for the court. He was appointed *Kirchenkomponist* (church composer) in 1746. In 1750 he was named vice-Kapellmeister under Hasse. His last work was a Mass in C dated 1752.

Santarelli, Giuseppe: (*b* Forli, 1710; *d* Rome, 1790). Italian castrato and composer. Active as an opera singer in Venice in the 1740s and later as a member of the Sistine Chapel Choir in Vatican City. He was appointed conductor of the latter in 1770.

Terradellas, Domingo Miguel Bernabe: (*b* Barcelona, 1711; *d* Rome, 20 May 1751). Italian composer of Spanish descent. He studied with Francesco Durante and produced operas for Turin, Venice, and Rome.

Veracini, Franceso Maria: (*b* Florence, 1 Feb 1690; *d* Florence, 31 Oct 1768). Italian composer and violinist. By July 1716, he was in Venice, where he dedicated a set of 12 solo sonatas to the Electoral Prince Friedrich August II of Saxony. The Prince persuaded his father to hire Veracini, even though there were no openings at the court for another violinist. Veracini was in the Prince's private employ from 25 January 1717, was put on the regular court payroll on 20 November

1717, and remained until 13 August 1722 when he suddenly left court, the professional jealousies aroused by his appointment having got the better of him.

Vinci, Leonardo: (*b* Strongoli, Calabria ?1696; *d* Naples, 27/28 May 1730). Italian composer, influential on composers such as Hasse, Handel, Pergolesi, and Vivaldi.

Wagenseil, Georg Christoph: (*b* Vienna, 29 Jan 1715; *d* Vienna, 1 March 1777). Austrian composer, keyboardist, and teacher. Appointed as composer to the court on 6 February 1739, a post he held until his death. Also served as organist from 1741 to 1750 in the private chapel of Empress Elisabeth Christine (widow of Charles VI) from 1741 until 1750, and in 1749 became *Hofklaviermeiste*r to the imperial Archduchesses.

The composers whose information is still hidden in some archive somewhere are **Scholari** and **Vicentino**.

BIBLIOGRAPHY

On Maria Antonia

Drewes, Heinz. *Maria Antonia Walpurgis als Komponistin.* (PhD diss, Universität Köln, 1934).

Fischer, Christine. "Selbststilisierungs- und Herrschaftskonzepte in Maria Antonia Walpurgis' *Talestri, regina delle amazzoni"* (unpublished article, 1999).

Fürstenau, Moritz. "Maria Antonia Walpurgis, Kurfürstin von Sachsen. Eine biographische Skizze," in M*onatshefte für Musikgeschichte* 11, Nr. 10 (1879), 167-187.

Gutschmidt, Christian Gotthelf von. *Ihre Churfürstlichen Durchlaucht zu Sachsen rechtsbegründete Ansprüche an die Bayerische Alloidal-Verlassenschaft mit Beylagen.* (Dresden, 1778).

Lippert, Woldemar. *Kaiserin Maria Theresia und Kurfürstin Maria*

Antonia von Sachsen: Briefwechsel 1747-1772. (Leipzig: G. B. Teubner, 1908).

McLamore, Alyson. "Princess Royal of Saxony, Maria Antonia Walpurgis." in: *Women Composers: Music Through the Ages*, Martha Furman Schleifer and Sylvia Glickman, eds. Vol 5. (New York: G. K. Hall, 1998).

Petzholdt, Julius. "Biographisch-litterarische Mittheilungen über Maria Antonia Walpurgis von Sachsen," in: *Neuer Anzeiger für Bibliographie und Bibliothekswissenschaft* 11 (1856), pp. 336-345, 367-390.

_____. *Maria Antonia Walpurgis. Kurfürstin von Sachsen, Geb. Prinzessin von Bayern* (Dresden, 1856).

Raab, Heribert. "Die Romreise der Kurfürsten-Witwe Maria Antonia Walpurgis von Sachsen 1772," in *Hundert Jahre deutsches Priesterkolleg beim Campo Santo Teutonico 1876-1976*, Erwin Gatz, editor. (Rome, 1977).

Schaal, Dieter. "Die Leibwaffen der Kurfürstin Maria Antonia im Historischen Museum, Dresden." in *Kunst und Antiquitäten*. 1992, 10, pp 51-55.

von Weber, Carl. *Maria Antonia Walpurgis, Churfürstin zu Sachsen, geb. Kaiserliche Prinzessin in Bayern*. (Dresden: B. G. Teubner, 1857).

Yorke-Long, Alan. *Music at Court: Four Eighteenth Century Studies.* (London: Weidenfeld and Nicolson, 1954).

[Unknown Author]. *Maria Antonia, Churfürstin zu Sachsen.* In: Wissenschaftl. Beil. der Leipziger Zeitung. Nr 66, 67, 68, August 1857.

House of Wettin and the Dresden court

Albert Herzog zu Sachsen. *Die Wettiner in Lebensbildern.* (Graz, Austria: Styria, 1995).

Ciancio, Valentina. *Pietro Graf Rotari in Dresden: Ein italienischer Maler am Hof König Augustus III.* (Dresden: Imorde, 1999).

Engelhardt, A. M. *Friedrich Christian, Churfürst von Sachsen. Ein biograph. Entwurf.* (Dresden: Wagner, 1828).

Löffler, Fritz. *Das alte Dresden.* (Leipzig: E. A. Seemann, 1999).

Paul, Martin. *Graf Wackerbarth-Salmour, Oberhofmeister des sächsischen Kurprinzen Friedrich Christian.* (Leipzig: von S. Hirzel, 1912).

Philippi, Hans. *Die Wettiner in Sachsen und Thüringen.* (Limburg: C. A. Starke, 1989).

Pölitz, Karl Heinrich Ludwig. *Die Regierung Friedrich Augusts,*

Königs von Sachsen. (Leipzig: J. C. Hinrichsschen Buchhandlung, 1830).

Schlechte, Horst. *Das geheime politische Tagebuch des Kurprinzen Friedrich Christian 1751 bis 1757.* (Weimar: Hermann Böhlaus Nachfolger, 1992).

Schmidt, Werner and Dirk Syndram, eds. *Unter einer Krone: Kunst und Kultur der sächsich-polnischen Union.* (Leipzig: Edition Leipzig, 1997).

Staszewski, Jacek. *August III. Kurfürst von Sachsen und König von Polen. Eine Biographie. Aus dem Polnischen von Eduard Merian.* (Berlin: Akademischer Verlag, 1996).

Tauscher, Katrin. *Das Stadtarchiv Dresden und seine Bestände.* (Dresden: Stadtarchiv, 1994).

House of Wittelsbach and the Munich court

Bekh, Wolfgang Johannes. *Ein Wittelsbacher in Italien.* (Munich: Bruckmann, 1971).

Elhardt, Rudolf. *Max III. Joseph: Kurfürst zwischen Rokoko und Aufklärung.* (Munich: Ehrenwirth, 1996).

Glaser, Hubert. *Wittelsbach: Kurfürsten im Reich—Könige von Bayern.* (Munich: Hirmer, 1993).

_____. *Kurfürst Max Emanuel: Bayern und Europa um 1700.* (Munich: Hirmer, 1976).

Hojer, Gerhard and Elmar D. Schmid. *Nymphenburg.* (Munich: Bayerische Verwaltung der staatlichen Schlösser, Gärten und See, 1999).

Lepage, Auguste. *Mémoire de l'Election de l'Empereur Charles VII.* (Paris: Academie des Bibliophiles, 1870).

Rall, Hans and Marga Rall. *Die Wittelsbacher von Otto I. bis Elisabeth I.* (Vienna: Tosa, 1997).

Straub, Eberhard. *Die Wittelsbacher.* (Berlin: Siedler, 1994).

Strauven, Dietmar. *Die Wittelsbachischen Familienverträge 1761-1779.* (PhD. Diss, Universität Köln, 1969).

Music and Culture, Germany and Holy Roman Empire

Bücken, Ernst. *München als Musikstadt.* (Hildburghausen: F. W. Gadow & Sohn, c 1923).

Buelow, George J. "Dresden in the Age of Absolutism" in *The Late Baroque Era from 1680-1740*, George J. Buelow, editor. (Englewood Cliffs: Prentice Hall, 1993).

Burney, Charles. *An Eighteenth-century Musical Tour in Central Europe and the Netherlands,* Percy A. Scholes, editor. (London: Oxford U, 1959).

Fürstenau, Moritz. "Beiträge zur Geschichte der Musik und des Theaters am sächsischen Hof während der Regierung Augusts III. 1733-1763," *Wissenschaftliche Beilage der Leipziger Zeitung* zu 88 (2.11.1856), 469-502.

_____. *Zur Geschichte der Musik und des Theaters am Hofe zu Dresden.* (Original edition: Dresden, 1861-1862. Reprint: Frankfurt a. M.: Peters, 1971).

Gagliardo, John. *Germany Under the Old Regime 1600-1790.* (London and New York: Longman, 1991).

_____. *Reich and Nation: The Holy Roman Empire as Idea and Reality, 1763-1806.* (Bloomington: Indiana University, 1980).

Gottsched, Johann Christoph, ed. *Sammlung einiger ausgesuchten Stücke, der Gesellschaft der freyen Künste zu Leipzig.* (Leipzig: Breitkopf, 1756).

Jaacks, Gisela and Carsten Prange. *Zeremoniell und Freiheit: Europa im 18 Jahrhundert — Die Welt des Johann Adolf Hasse* (Bremen: W. Zertani, 1999).

Landmann, Ortrun. *Die Dresdner italienische Oper zwischen Hasse und Weber.* (Dresden: Sächsishe Landesbibliothek, 1989).

_____. *Die Telemann-Quellen der Sächsischen Landesbibliothek: Handschriften und zeitgenössische Druckausgaben seiner Werke.* (Dresden: Sächsische Landesbibliothek, 1990).

_____. "Gli amanti folletti- ein Dresdener Mozart-Pasticcio" in Renate Herklotz, Renate Schaaf, and Karl-Heinz Kohler, eds. *Kongressbericht zum VII Internationalen Gewandhaus-Sympossium: Wolfgang Amadeus Mozart Forschung und Praxis im Dienst von Leben, Werk, Interpretation und Rezeption anlasslich der Gewandhaus-Festtage in Leipzig vom 3. Bis 6. Oktober 1991.* (Leipzig: Peters, 1993).

_____. *Katalog der Dresdener Hasse-Musikhandschriften.* (Munich: K. G. Saur, 1999).

Legband, Paul. *Münchener Bühne und Litteratur im achtzehnten Jahrhundert.* (Munich: Historischen Vereins von Oberbayern, 1904).

Sheehan, James J. *German History, 1770-1866.* (New York and Oxford: Oxford University Press, 1989).

Umbach, Maiken. *Federalism and Enlightenment in Germany 1740-1806.* (London: Hamledon Press, 2000).

Music and Culture, Italy

Brunelli, Bruno. *Tutte le Opere di Pietro Metastasio. Vols I-V.* (Milan: A. Mondadori, 1943-1954).

Bucciarelli, Melania. *Italian Opera and European Theatre, 1680-1720.* (Turnhout: Brepols, 2000).

Cattelan, Paolo. "Giovanni Ferrandini, Musicista 'Padovano'." in *Mozart, Padova e la Betulia liberata: Committenza, interpretazione e fortuna delle azioni sacre metastasiane nel '700.* (Florence: Olschki, 1991).

Colzani, Alberto, Norbert Dubowy, Andrea Luppi and Maurizio Padoan eds. *Il melodramma italiano in Italia e in Germania nell'età barocca.* (Como: AMIS, 1995).

Giorgetti-Vichi, Anna Maria. *Gli Arcadi dal 1690 al 1800.* (Rome: Arcadia Accademia Letteraria Italiana, 1977).

Lee, Vernon. [Paget, Violet]. *Studies of the Eighteenth Century in Italy.* (London: T. Fisher Unwin, 1887).

Massaro, Maria Nevila. "Il ballo pantomimo al Teatro Nuovo di Padova." in *Acta Musicologica,* Vol LVII/2 (1985), 215-75.

Strohm, Reinhard. *Dramma per Musica: Italian Opera Seria of the Eighteenth Century.* (New Haven: Yale University Press, 1997).

The Nobility and Court Life

Elias, Norbert. *The Court Society.* (New York: Pantheon, 1983).

Rogalla von Bieberstein, Johannes. *Adelsherrschaft und Adelskultur in Deutschland.* (Limburg: C. A. Starke, 1998).

Pastoral

Gifford, Terry. *Pastoral.* (London: Routledge, 1999).

Greg, Walter W. *Pastoral Poetry and Pastoral Drama.* (New York: Russell & Russell, 1959).

Guarini, Battista (1590). *Il Pastor Fido.*

_____. *Il Pastor Fido.* Translated by Dr. Thomas Sheridan (c. 1730). Edited and Completed by Robert Hogan and Edward A. Nickerson. (London: Associated University Presses, 1989).

Harris, Ellen T. *Handel and the Pastoral Tradition.* (London: Oxford University Press, 1980).

Tasso, Torquato (1573). *Aminta.*

Vocal Performance and Performance Practice

Agricola, J. H. (1757) *Anleitung zur Singkunst* (Reprint: Celle: Hermann Moeck, 1966).

Barnett, Dene. *The Art of Gesture: The practices and principles of 18th century acting.* (Heidelberg: Carl Winter, 1987).

Christiansen, Rupert. *Prima Donna: A History.* (New York: Viking, 1985).

Coffin, Berton. *Historical Vocal Pedagogy Classics.* (Metuchen, NJ: Scarecrow Press, 1989).

Cone, Edward T. *The Composer's Voice.* (Berkeley: University of California, 1974).

Fuller, David. "The Performer as Composer." in: Howard Mayer Brown and Stanley Sadie, eds. *Performance Practice: Music after 1600.* (London: Macmillan Press, 1989).

Harris, Ellen. "Voices" in: Howard Mayer Brown and Stanley Sadie, eds. *Performance Practice: Music after 1600.* (London: Macmillan Press, 1989).

Quantz, Johann Joachim. *On Playing the Flute.* Translated and annotated by Edward R. Reilly. (New York: Schirmer, 1985).

Rosand, Ellen. "Barbara Strozzi, virtuosissima cantatrice: the composer's voice." in *Journal of the American Musicological Society,* Vol XXXI/2 (Summer 1978), 241-81.

Roselli, John. *Singers of Italian Opera: The History of a Profession.* (Cambridge, UK: Cambridge University Press, 1992).

Tosi, Pier Francesco (1743). *Observations on the Florid Song.* Translated and annotated by Gaillard. J. Wilcox, London. (Reprint: Johnson Reprint, 1968).

Women in Music, Literature and History

Armstrong, Isobel and Virginia Blain. *Women's Poetry in the Enlightenment.* (London: Macmillan, 1999).

Baldauf-Berdes, Jane L. *Women Musicians of Venice: Musical Foundations, 1525-1855.* (Oxford: Clarendon, 1996).

Bannet, Eve Tavor. *The Domestic Revolution: Enlightenment Feminisms and the Novel.* (Baltimore: Johns Hopkins, 2000).

Blackwell, Jeannine and Susanne Zantop. *Bitter Healing: German Women Writers from 1700 to 1830* (Lincoln, Nebraska: University of Nebraska, 1990).

Bowers, Jane and Judith Tick. *Women Making Music: The Western Art Tradition, 1150-1950* (Chicago: University of Illinois Press, 1987).

Citron, Marcia J. *Gender and the Musical Canon.* (Cambridge, UK: Cambridge University Press, 1993).

Cook, Susan C. and Judy S. Tsou. *Cecilia Reclaimed: Feminist Perspectives on Gender and Music.* (Urbana and Chicago: University of Illinois Press, 1994).

Davis, Natalie Zemon and Arlette Farge, eds. *A History of Women in the West, vol 3 Renaissance and Enlightenment Paradoxes.* (Cambridge, MA: Harvard University Press, 1993).

Dawson, Ruth. "Frauen und Theater. Vom Stegreifspiel zum bürgerlichen Rührstück." in *Deutsche Literatur von Frauen,* Gisela Brinker-Gabler, editor. Bd. 1. (Munich: C. H. Beck, 1988).

Freeman, Daniel E. "La guerriera amante: Representations of Amazons and Warrior Queens in Venetian Baroque Opera." in *Musical Quarterly* 53, Nr. 3 (Fall 1996), 431-460 (447-448).

French, Lorely, *German Women as Letter Writers: 1750-1850.* (London: Associated University Presses, 1996).

Goodman, Katherine R. *Amazons and Apprentices: Women and the German Parnassus in the Early Enlightenment.* (New York: Camden House, 1999).

Gottsched, Luise Adelgunde. *Pietism in Petticoats and Other*

Comedies. Translated by Thomas Kerth and John R. Russell. (Columbia, SC: Camden House, 1994).

Hufton, Olwen. *The Prospect Before Her: A History of Women in Western Europe 1500-1800.* (New York: A. A. Knopf, 1996).

Jackson, Barbara Garvey. *'Say Can You Deny Me': A Guide to Surviving Music by Women from the 16th through the 18th Centuries.* (Fayetteville: University of Arkansas Press, 1994).

Jezic, Diane and Elizabeth Wood. *Women Composers: The Lost Tradition Found.* (New York: The Feminist Press, 1988).

Jones, Vivien, ed. *Women in the Eighteenth Century: Constructions of Femininity.* (London: Routledge, 1990).

Kord, Susanne. *Little Detours: The Letters and Plays of Luise Gottsched (1713-1762).* (New York: Camden House, 2000).

Koskoff, Ellen, ed. *Women and Music in Cross-Cultural Perspective* (New York: Greenwood, 1987).

Marshall, Kimberly, ed. *Rediscovering the Muses: Women's Musical Traditions.* (Boston: Northeastern University Press, 1993).

Neuls-Bates, Carol. *Women in Music* (Boston: Northeastern University, 1996).

Petschauer, Peter. *The Education of Women in Eighteenth-Century Germany: New Directions from the German Female Perspective* (Lewiston: E. Mellen Press, 1989).

von Runckel, Dorothee Henriette, ed. *Briefe der Frau Adelgunde Victorie Gottsched geborne Kalmus* (Dresden: Harpeter, 1771).

Sadie, Julie Anne & Rhian Samuel. *The Norton/Grove Dictionary of Women Composers.* (New York: W. W. Norton, 1995).

Solie, Ruth, ed. *Musicology and Difference: Gender and Sexuality in Music Scholarship.* (Los Angeles: University of California Press, 1993).

Music History

Le Huray, Peter and James Day. *Music and Aesthetics in the Eighteenth and Early Nineteenth Centuries.* (Cambridge, UK: Cambridge University Press, 1981).

Sadie, Julie Anne, ed. *Companion to Baroque Music.* (Berkeley and Los Angeles: University of California Press, 1990).

Sadie, Stanley, ed. *The New Grove Dictionary of Opera.* (London: Macmillan, 1992).

_____. *The New Grove Dictionary of Music and Musicians.* (London: Macmillan, 2001).

Salmen, Walther. *The Social Status of the Professional Musician* (New York: Pendragon Press, 1983).

Sartori, Claudio. *I libretti italiani a stampa dalle origini al 1800.* (Cuneo: Bertola & Locatelli, 1990).

Internet Sources

Britannica, The Editors of Encyclopaedia. "Pompeo Girolamo Batoni". *Encyclopedia Britannica*, https://www.britannica.com/biography/Pompeo-Girolamo-Batoni. Accessed 23 Jan. 2023.

de Brie, Tim. https://composers-classical-music.com/. Accessed 23 Jan. 2023.

PHOTO CREDITS

Image of the painting by Rotari, *Maria Antonia of Bavaria (1724-1780), wife of Elector Friedrich Christian of Saxony* © Gemäldegalerie Alte Meister, Staatliche Kunstsammlungen Dresden. Photo: Elke Estel/ Hans-Peter Klut

All other illustrations are scans or photos of primary sources by the author of this work.

Author Bio

Dr. April Lynn James is an award-winning soprano and scholar. She is sought after as a speaker on the connection between creativity, spirituality, and wellness. For over a decade, she has been inspiring others through **April plus Madison,** her latest entrepreneurial venture.

She had the distinguished honor of studying abroad in Dresden, Germany, courtesy of a **DAAD** (Deutscher Akademischer Austauschdienst/German Academic Exchange Service) **Fellowship**, where she researched the music and life of Maria Antonia, Electress of Saxony.

Dr. April founded **The Maria Antonia Project**, an opera company whose mission is to bring operas composed by women out of the archives and onto the stage. A groundbreaking researcher in the area of Women in Music, her exhibitions, *In Her Own Hand: Operas Composed by Women 1625-1913* (Harvard Music Library) and *Women Composing for Marian Anderson* (Penn Libraries), were enthusiastically received, and she is sought after as a speaker on this subject. Her research on Marian Anderson became part of the recent *American Masters* documentary, *Marian Anderson: The Whole World in Her Hands*, directed by Emmy- and Peabody Award-winner Rita Coburn.

It was the Tim Burton film, *Alice in Wonderland* (2010), that took Dr. April down the rabbit hole and led to her guardian angel, Madison Hatta, Sonneteer, springing full-blown into her consciousness. Madison's chapbooks, the *Book of Unreasonable Rhymes* (2015) and the *Book of Unrelenting Rhymes* (2016) are available from Philadelphia's legendary Moonstone Press.

Dr. April holds a PhD in Music from Harvard University, as well as degrees from Queens College of the City University of New York and Drexel University.

But Wait, There's More!

I hope you've enjoyed getting to know Maria Antonia and her world better. If you'd like to continue the journey, download the free PDF, *Maria Antonia's Dresden (and Munich)*. In it, you will find links to images of people and places that will help you to visualize the world Her Highness inhabited more than mere words ever can. Click here to download.

<https://april-plus-madison.newzenler.com/f/maria-antonia-s-dresden-and-munich>

Positive poetry anyone? A sampling of Wonderland-inspired, whimsical rhymes declaimed by my guardian angel, Madison Hatta, Sonneteer, may be heard here. Enjoy!

For those listening to the book, go to https://soundcloud.com/alj-1-1/sets/aprilplusmadisonsa-musings.

Looking for a Wonderland-inspired, whimsical gift for others or for yourself? Check out **April plus Madison's Whimsicali-Tea Shop** on Zazzle: https://www.zazzle.com/store/april_plus_madison/products

Love This Book?
Leave a Review!

Shout it from the rooftops. Tattle about it over tea! Now head over to Amazon (or wherever you purchased this book) to leave a review. It will only take two minutes of your time.

You can also leave a review on my website:

https://www.aprillynnjames.com/tenth-muse-reviews

Every review matters, and it matters *a lot!*

Your feedback will help me know in which direction to go for my (plus Madison's) next books and projects.

With Gra-Tea-tude,

April (plus Madison)

Self-Publishing School

NOW IT'S YOUR TURN

Discover the EXACT 3-step blueprint you need to become a bestselling author in as little as 3 months.

Self-Publishing School helped me, and now I want them to help you with this FREE resource to begin outlining your book!

Even if you're busy, bad at writing, or don't know where to start, you CAN write a bestseller and build your best life.

With tools and experience across a variety of niches and professions, Self-Publishing School is the <u>only</u> resource you need to take your book to the finish line!

DON'T WAIT

Say "YES" to becoming a bestseller:

https://self-publishingschool.com/friend/

Follow the steps on the page to get a FREE resource to get started on your book and unlock a discount to get started with Self-Publishing School.

www.ingramcontent.com/pod-product-compliance
Lightning Source LLC
Chambersburg PA
CBHW071715120626
46550CB00001B/242